LINKING
YOUR
BEADS

LINKING YOUR BEADS

The Rosary's History, Mysteries, and Prayers

by PATRICIA ANN KASTEN

Our Sunday Visitor Publishing Division
Our Sunday Visitor, Inc.
Huntington, Indiana 46750

Nihil Obstat
Msgr. Michael Heintz, Ph.D.
Censor Librorum

Imprimatur
✠ Kevin C. Rhoades
Bishop of Fort Wayne-South Bend
November 19, 2010

The *Nihil Obstat* and *Imprimatur* are official declarations that a book is free from doctrinal or moral error. It is not implied that those who have granted the *Nihil Obstat* and *Imprimatur* agree with the contents, opinions, or statements expressed.

CONTENTS

CHAPTER I

From the Desert to Dominicans

In a good garden, you find yourself surrounded by myriad plants, flowers and trees, sunlight and birdsong. It's a world apart, yet firmly within the everyday world. Likewise, as Catholics, we are surrounded by myriad images of our Faith: chants and chapels, spoken prayers and bended knees, candles and incense, stained glass and sprinkled water.

But few images of the Catholic faith are more enduring than a simple string of beads.

Whether wrapped around our grandfather's fingers, swinging from the waist of a sister in full habit, or dangling in the sun from a rearview mirror, Rosary beads have encircled our lives. An image of Rosary beads brings to mind not only prayer but also images from a lifetime of prayers, arranged like scattered flowers in our lives.

The Rosary, as a formal devotional prayer, is about 500–600 years old. However, its roots go back to the desert, where the early monastic mothers and fathers withdrew to devote themselves to prayer. And the Rosary shares branches with other religions, such as Islam and Buddhism, which have used prayer beads and prayer ropes for centuries.

Looking simply at the Rosary beads themselves, we learn that they were named from the Latin word *rosarium*, meaning a garland of roses. Like a flower garland, the Rosary is a physical thing; it's an actual prayer tool that serves to remind us of which prayers to pray and when, and helps us keep count of those prayers, which makes meditation easier. Our fingers keep count while our minds turn to contemplation.

The most familiar Rosary form, with its total of 150 Hail Marys, reflects the 150 psalms and grew out of the liturgical practice of daily recitation of those psalms. Or, more correctly, it grew out of *not* being able to say all the psalms every day. Or on any day.

Sometimes called the "poor man's breviary," the Rosary with its repeated prayers grew in popularity just as Latin died out as a read and spoken language. Literacy in general declined across Europe during the Middle Ages, and the practice appeared of substituting repeated familiar prayers with the no-longer-familiar psalms. Either one Lord's Prayer (the Our Father) or one *Ave* (the Hail Mary) was substituted for the recitation of each psalm, totaling 150 prayers. A string of beads kept count of the prayers, and the Rosary sprouted into existence.

During the centuries that followed the Middles Ages, people continued to attend Mass, but were less and less called upon to actively participate in that Mass. This led many of the faithful to turn to private prayer, reciting the Rosary while the priest "said the Mass." Until almost the day she died, my grandmother carried a Rosary to Mass, fingering its beads and mouthing those familiar prayers during the homily and the Eucharistic prayer.

The most familiar Rosary consists of five sets of ten beads (called a decade), separated by five other beads. Other forms of the Rosary, sometimes called chaplets, consist of seven, fifteen, or even twenty decades on one string. There are even double rosaries, linked together. Each has an attached pendant consisting of a crucifix and beads. The crucifix, the central medallion, the big beads, and the small beads all signify different prayers and different mysteries. Here we find the Apostles' Creed, the Lord's Prayer, the Glory Be, the recently added *Salve Regina* and, of course, the Hail Mary. Certain other prayers, including the Fatima Prayers, may be added, but are not necessary to complete a Rosary.

This common five-decade form of the Rosary, called "the Dominican Rosary," is often credited to St. Dominic, the founder of the Dominican order, who lived from 1170–1221. Pious tradition says that Dominic received the Rosary from the Virgin Mary herself sometime between 1206 and 1214. However, actual evidence of the full Rosary devotion being practiced only traces back to about the fifteenth century.

While various sources[1] note this lack of a direct connection between Dominic and the Rosary, there are documents written about Rosary devotions by several Dominican preachers between

1220 and 1450. Certainly, it is the Dominicans we can thank for much of the spread of the Rosary devotion across Europe. A great deal of that credit goes to a Dominican preacher, Blessed Alanus de Rupe (Alan de la Roche) — sometimes called the Apostle of the Rosary — who promoted the devotion later in the fifteenth century.

Another St. Dominic is also connected to the growth of the Rosary: Dominic of Prussia, a Carthusian monk who lived in the same century as Blessed Alan. This Dominic developed a form of meditation upon the mysteries of Christ, using 150 Hail Marys, that is sometimes called the "Life of Jesus Rosary."

But whatever the truth about these early centuries in the development of the Rosary, we can definitely thank a saintly pope, who was a Dominican, for today's prominence of the Rosary.

In 1566, Cardinal Ghislieri, a Dominican priest who had taken the religious name of Michele, became Pope Pius V. Even before his papal election, Pius V figured prominently in the Counter-Reformation: he was the pope who excommunicated Elizabeth I of England in 1570.

Pius V was devoted to the Rosary and believed it had power to overcome the heresies that were threatening the Church at the time. In 1569, he issued the papal bull *Consueverunt Romani Pontifices*, which promoted the Rosary as a weapon of spiritual warfare and for use in personal renewal and conversion.

Pius V, who was canonized in 1712, was not the only pope devoted to the Rosary. Others included Leo XIII, Blessed John XXIII, Pope Paul VI, and Venerable Pope John Paul II, who made the significant addition of the five Luminous Mysteries to the Rosary in 2002.

Today, people still use the Rosary — as they have done for centuries — to meditate upon the mystery of salvation, as revealed through key events in the lives of Jesus and Mary. There are now twenty mysteries of the Rosary, divided into four groups:

- **The Joyful Mysteries** consist of the Annunciation, the Visitation, the Nativity, the Presentation, and the Finding of the Child Jesus in the Temple. This set of mysteries helps us reflect on the beginnings of our salvation as seen in the events of the Incarnation.

- **The Luminous Mysteries** were added by Pope John Paul II on October 16, 2002, with his apostolic letter on the Rosary, *Rosarium Virginis Mariae*. Drawing on the work of Blessed George Preca in 1957, the pope chose to add five "mysteries of light" that focused on Jesus's public life. The five are the Baptism in the Jordan, the Wedding at Cana, the Proclamation of the Kingdom, the Transfiguration, and the Last Supper.
- **The Sorrowful Mysteries** are the Agony in the Garden, the Scourging at the Pillar, the Crowning with Thorns, the Carrying of the Cross, and the Crucifixion. These help to focus our thoughts on the redemptive suffering and death of Jesus.
- **The Glorious Mysteries** are the Resurrection, the Ascension, the Descent of the Holy Spirit, the Assumption of Mary, and the Crowning of Mary as Queen of Heaven. These mysteries focus on the glorification of Jesus — and, through him, Mary — and the salvation hope of all the Church.

While these twenty mysteries are the most common form of the Rosary, there really is no "correct" way to say a Rosary, just as there is no "correct" way to plant a garden, though the end result is the same. Recitation of the Rosary varies between cultures and countries and has evolved over the centuries with various forms of the Rosary, longer or shorter, being used for different prayer purposes.

The key purpose, however, of any Rosary or chaplet remains the same: to help us to meditate upon the wonders of our salvation and the glory of new life won for us through Christ.

CHAPTER 2

The Pitter-Patter of Lady Godiva

While the Rosary as we know it today did not come into widespread use until the fourteenth and fifteenth centuries, prayer beads have a longer tradition.

Strings of beads used for prayer date back to earliest times. *The Catholic Encyclopedia* mentions a statue from the ancient Assyrian city of Nineveh (now in Iraq) that was adorned with prayer beads.[2] Nineveh was at its height of power in the seventh century B.C., long before the traditional thirteenth-century advent of the Rosary.

The oldest prayer beads that can be accurately traced as prayer aids come from the Hindu religion, which dates back some 2,500 years to ancient India. *Japa mala* (from "*japa*," meaning "a repetitive prayer, " and "*mala*," meaning "a garland of flowers," often roses) are strings of prayer beads, sometimes worn around the neck. They consist of 108 beads used for repeating mantras, words taken from the Sanskrit language — often prayers and names of various deities.

Buddhism, which developed out of Hinduism around the fourth century B.C. under the teachings of Siddhārtha Gautama (the Enlightened One, or the Buddha), also uses the *japa mala*. In China, prayer beads are often called *shu zhu*, meaning "counting beads," since they are used to count prayers.

Today, members of most modern religions use prayer beads, including Catholics, Orthodox Christians, Muslims, Hindus, and Buddhists. Jews do not; however, they do place intricate knots at the ends of their prayer shawls, and these serve a similar purpose as aids in the recitation of prayers. Even Anglicans use prayer beads — a practice that started very recently (in the 1980s); thirty-three beads, representing the years Christ was on earth, with prayers attached to their use.

Lutherans also have recently begun to use a "rosary" during Lenten meditations.

Muslim prayer beads consist of ninety-nine beads, for each of the ninety-nine names of Allah found in the Koran, and sometimes have the addition of a "leader bead." (These have been incorrectly labeled as "worry beads" by non-Muslims.) Muslim prayer beads are used in the process known as *tasbih*, a repetition of prayers that give glory to God. Called *misbaha*, the prayer beads, which may have developed from customs of the Persians, date to the time of Mohammed (A.D. 570–632). Some *misbaha* are only thirty-three beads in length and are used three times through to complete the names.

True Christian prayer beads date to the desert fathers and mothers — the founders of what we now know as monastic life in the third and fourth centuries — who lived as hermits in order to be closer to God. The desert mothers and fathers made a practice of praying the 150 psalms daily. To keep count of their prayers, many used pebbles kept in a bag or bowl. This prayer custom of reciting the psalms is sometimes called the Davidic Psalter, in honor of King David, the traditional author of the psalms.

St. Anthony of Egypt and St. Pachomius (both of whom lived in the fourth century) are the desert fathers most often credited with developing prayer ropes, the direct ancestors of the Rosary. These prayer ropes consisted of strings of leather tied with 50 or 150 knots, so that the psalms could be counted more easily — and with less weight than a bowl of 150 pebbles.

As time passed, these desert monks were joined by followers who could not read, and the practice of substituting other prayers for the 150 psalms was made to accommodate those who could not memorize the psalms. The Lord's Prayer, not the Hail Mary, was the most frequent substitute.

This practice of using a prayer rope with the Lord's Prayer persisted in the Western church until the Marian version gained popularity in the fourteenth and fifteenth centuries. Indeed, thanks to this prayerful repetition of the Lord's Prayer, we have the origin of the phrase "pitter patter" — a derivation of the word "patter" which developed in the fourteenth century from the English word "*patren*." The word referred to and what many heard in the local churches as the monks and nuns repeatedly whispered the Latin *Pater Noster* prayer: "*Pater Noster, qui es in caelis* …"

In the Eastern Church, the prayer rope of the desert hermits persists to this day, largely unchanged. Called *komboskini* in Greek (literally, "a rope with knots") and *chotki* in Russian, these prayer ropes are traditionally made of wool — to symbolize the Good Shepherd — and consist of 33, 50, or 100 knots. Instead of the Lord's Prayer or the Hail Mary, however, Orthodox Christians use the rope to repeat the Jesus Prayer: "Jesus Christ, Son of God, have mercy on me, a sinner."

In the West, the European-based Rosary continued to use the Our Father prayer rope. We know this from records of multiple *Paters* kept by religious communities by the turn of the first millennium. The *Ancient Customs of Cluny*, compiled in 1096, note that repetitions of the Lord's Prayer — or of fifty psalms — were offered by nonordained brothers upon the death of a fellow member, just as priests of the order offered fifty memorial Masses. Also, eighth-century "penitentials," rule books that guided confessors in dealing with penitents, prescribed various penances of twenty, fifty, or more *Paters*. The *Pater Noster* prayer ropes became aids in these penances and offerings.

Besides those in religious life and the priesthood, lay people came to use prayer beads as well. One famous example showing a link between prayer beads and Marian devotion is the story of Lady Godiva (*Godgifu*) — yes, the same lady of naked horseback lore immortalized by Alfred Lord Tennyson. Godiva was a real woman who lived in Coventry, England, in the eleventh century. She was Countess of Mercia and very concerned about the poor — whose unfair taxation led to her ride of protest. According to William of Malmesbury, a monk historian of the twelfth century, the countess's will (she died in 1070) donated a string of precious stones to adorn a statue of Mary probably located at a religious house for which she and her husband had donated land in Coventry in 1040.

CHAPTER 3

The Power Tools of Contemplation

The knots and beads we know today as rosaries began as 150 pebbles sitting in a bowl in a monk's hut in the desert. And those pebbles, though transformed into a bead rosary today, still give us an idea of what meditative prayer is all about in Church tradition.

St. Paul wrote in the letter to the Thessalonians that we should "pray without ceasing" (1 Thessalonians 5:17). The Davidic Psalter — reciting 150 Psalms — is one way to do that, as the desert fathers and mothers did in the second century. Another is the Rosary.

We can often tend to think of prayer as something we only do at certain times — before and after meals or at bedtime — or in certain places, like a church or chapel. And yet, the Rosary's portability tells us that it is meant go anywhere, and to be used at any time. That makes it the perfect tool for meditative, or contemplative, prayer.

Repetitive prayers, like 150 Our Father on prayer ropes and Hail Mary on rosaries, help us keep focused — they quiet our minds and direct our thoughts to God.

Contemplative prayer is a meditative form of prayer, done in silence, with the express desire of placing one's self in the presence of God. The word "contemplation" means just that; the Latin words from which it derives — *con templare* — mean "to be with, in the temple," or to refer to a "place to read auguries."

ST. ANTHONY OF EGYPT

Many of us may think of meditation as a form of Eastern mysticism, but as we have seen, it is rooted in early Christianity and the desert monastics. St. Anthony of Egypt (251–356) exemplifies those desert fathers and mothers who became hermits so that they could be alone with God and pray constantly. What people like Anthony found is that meditation engages the entire person in prayer, allowing us to tie ourselves more closely to Christ.

As the *Catechism of the Catholic Church* tells us:

> Meditation engages thought, imagination, emotion, and desire. This mobilization of faculties is necessary in order to deepen our convictions of faith, prompt the conversion of our heart, and strengthen our will to follow Christ. Christian prayer tries above all to meditate on the mysteries of Christ, as in *lectio divina* (an ancient form of prayer and meditation involving the Scriptures) or the Rosary.
>
> — No. 2708

It further adds that reflecting on the mysteries of Christ in prayer is meant to lead us into personal knowledge of the love that Jesus has for us, and the union to which he wishes to draw us.

The purpose of meditative prayer, as St. Anthony is often quoted, is to "always have God before your eyes." This is not easy to do. Too many things, people, activities, and thoughts distract us. And few of us can go away to the desert and become hermits like Anthony — even though we may long to do so! So instead, we can sometimes despair of ever being able to "pray unceasingly" and come to think that contemplative prayer and meditation are beyond us.

This is not true. While meditative prayer does involve stillness and silence, it also has an active dimension. And we have no better example of this than a saint tied to the Rosary: St. Joseph.

JOSEPH

Joseph was a man who worked with his hands — and was found, not in the desert, but in the midst of the noise of a carpenter's workshop. Today, he would be working with power drills, saws, and nail guns. That's not the image of a man of silence. It's the image of a busy man, and Joseph was: he was a workman, a married man, a father. He traveled to Bethlehem, to Egypt, back to Nazareth, and frequently to Jerusalem, for the Passover and the other Jewish pilgrimage feasts.

Yet what is notable about Joseph is that, in the Gospels, he is really a man of silence. There is not one word attributed to him in the Scriptures. Silence surrounds him. Still, this is the man who heard angels speak in his dreams. He reflected on things, as we know he did when he found out Mary was with child. He was a righteous man, as Matthew (1:19) tells us. Clearly, he was a man of prayer.

The late Pope John Paul II, in his 1989 apostolic letter on Jesus's foster father, said:

> [Joseph's silence, even today,] is a silence that reveals, in a special way, the inner portrait of the man. The Gospels speak exclusively of what Joseph "did." Still, they allow us to discover in his "'actions'" — shrouded in silence as they are — an aura of deep contemplation.[3]

Silence and action: this gives us the image of the strong, silent type of man so often present in our fictional movies. But, for Christians, this strong, silent image belongs to a man who listened to angels, a man who prayed and meditated — even as he worked in the tasks of daily life.

And because he was open to God's word, even in his everyday tasks, Joseph heard that word spoken to him directly. The Gospels tell us that this happened four times, each time heralded by the appearance of an angel.

If you read the Gospel references of each of these four events, you can see that Joseph clearly meditated upon the word he received from God — thinking about it and weighing what he must do. Then, after such contemplation, Joseph acted. And he did so decisively.

- First, in the midst of preparing for married life, Joseph hears that Mary is pregnant. Clearly stunned by the news, Joseph made the difficult decision to divorce her quietly. But after the angel appeared (Matthew 1:18–24), he set aside his own plans and acted on God's word. He "took his wife into his home."

- Later, while caring for his new family in Bethlehem and having just entertained visitors from a far-off land, Joseph again heard an angel's warning. Without question and in the middle of the night, he rose from sleep, gathered his family, "and departed to Egypt" (Matthew 2:13–14), again listening to and acting in accord with God's word.

- Once again, after an undisclosed period of time in Egypt providing for his family, he heard the angel speak again. And Joseph, ever silent and ever attentive, "rose and took the child and his mother, and went to the land of Israel" (Matthew 2:21).

- And finally, fearful and indecisive about where to settle his family upon their return to the land of Israel, Joseph again heard God's message and moved to Galilee (Matthew 2:22–23).

In many ways, Joseph was just like any one of us: confused about his upcoming marriage, subject to government whim and taxes, needing to make a living to support himself and his family, and in search of a place to live. He reminds us of any average working person today, more than of any hermit in the desert. And yet, with his deep interior life, lived close to God — both before and after the Divine Child entered his household — Joseph does just what those desert hermits sought to do. He transforms those very ordinary moments of life into moments of prayer.

And that is the key to contemplative prayer, done in the pattern of St. Joseph.

In part, this silent way of action is why St. Teresa of Ávila recommended that anyone who needs someone to teach them how to pray should turn to Joseph.

Joseph had his personal tools and the life of Christ always before his eyes as he worked with those tools. As a man of prayer he, like his wife, must have "kept all these things, pondering on them in (his) heart" (Luke 2:19). And those heartfelt meditations led to his silent but faithful actions.

We also have our tools for doing the same thing — not a carpenter's tools, but the Gospels, showing us the life of Christ, and the Rosary beads.

MEDITATION

Meditation as a word comes from the same Latin roots as the word "medicine": *mederi*, which means "to remedy." As followers of Christ, we are called to direct our lives toward a constant attentiveness to God, both through praise and worship and by action and deed as ministers of God's healing presence. St. Joseph, who listened to angels and worked as a carpenter, offers us a perfect example that blends the sounds of saws with divine commands and brings us the prayer tools that can bring health to our lives.

CHAPTER 4

The Rosary's Older Cousin

In the same way Joseph kept God's word present in his life through reflection and meditation while he went about his daily work, so the desert fathers and mothers also kept God's word present to them through the work of their own hands.

In the tradition of the Church, one of the earliest prayer forms used for meditation — the knotted prayer rope — was first utilized to recite the 150 psalms. Later, the *Pater Noster*, the Lord's Prayer, was substituted. Finally, in the Eastern tradition of the Church, it was the Jesus Prayer that was repeated over the beads.

Today, for both Eastern rite Catholics and members of Orthodox churches, such a Jesus Prayer "prayer rope" consists of a cord with several knots, called a *komboskini* or *komboloi* in Greek (as mentioned previously). The monks on Mount Athos are known for these beads, even though these prayer ropes — or sets of prayer beads based on them — are also incorrectly called "worry beads" by those who do not understand their use.

THE JESUS PRAYER

The prayer said over this older cousin of the Rosary is shorter than even the *Ave* of the Hail Mary. Though both longer and shorter versions exist, the most frequently used form of this prayer is: "Lord Jesus Christ, Son of God, have mercy on me, a sinner."

Over and over again, the words are repeated until they become a rhythm in the mind of one who prays. To both Eastern rite Catholics and members of the Eastern Orthodox churches, the prayer is known as "The Prayer of the Heart," because they believe that both heart and mind are to be united when one approaches God.

Pope John Paul II called the Jesus Prayer "the soul's very breath" and said that by using the prayer we are "helped to feel the Savior's presence in everything (we) encounter."[4]

The Jesus Prayer is over fifteen centuries old. However, it was not well known in the Western church until it became popular with the publication of an anonymous nineteenth-century Russian work called *The Way of the Pilgrim*. The narrator prayed the prayer, using a prayer rope, as he travelled across Russia. The tale was translated into English in the early twentieth century. Later, when centering prayer became popular, the Jesus Prayer was rediscovered as an aid to that method of contemplative prayer.

The words of the Jesus Prayer derive from several instances in the Gospels where Jesus's help is requested. For example, in Matthew, two blind men plead, "Son of David, have pity on us!" (Matthew 9:27). And in Mark, Bartimaeus speaks the same words: "Son of David, have pity on me." (Mark 10:48). Luke also presents the words in a parable of Jesus, showing a tax collector going to the Temple to pray: "God, be merciful to me a sinner" (Luke 18:13).

The *Catechism of the Catholic Church* says that the Jesus Prayer reminds us that Jesus always responded to the simplest plea to heal infirmities and forgive sins, always responding as he did to the blind man, "Your faith has made you well; go in peace" (No. 2616).

A PROFESSION OF FAITH

The Jesus Prayer itself, though short, is actually a type of a creed — a simple profession of faith in Jesus Christ as the Son of God, able to dispense divine grace and mercy. The prayer contains three parts, each serving as a different focus for the prayer:

- "Lord Jesus Christ." The first part focuses on the Holy Name. Jesus's name, like all our names, has a meaning. Jesus, or *Yeshua* in Hebrew, means "savior" (the name given to him by an angel), and *Christos* means "the Anointed One" in Greek, a title of the Messiah. However, unlike any other name, Jesus's name is also the divine name, "the name which is above every name" (Phil 2:9–10). The sixth-century hermit, St. Barsanuphius the Great, called the unceasing invocation of this divine name "a medicine," working upon our souls in ways we cannot begin to understand.

- "Son of God." To voice this confession of faith opens us up to the working of the Holy Spirit, since, as Paul states, "No one can say 'Jesus is Lord' except by the Holy Spirit" (1 Corinthians 12:3). Saying these words in prayer serves to remind us that we are turning ourselves over to letting God work in our lives. It also leads to the third part of the prayer.
- "Have mercy on me, a sinner." Fr. Steven Peter Tsichlis, pastor of St. Paul's Greek Orthodox Church in Irvine, California, states that the Jesus Prayer helps us take the first step of a spiritual journey:

> . . . the recognition of our own sinfulness, our essential estrangement from God and the people around us. The Jesus Prayer is a prayer in which we admit our desperate need of a Savior.[5]

The Jesus Prayer is simple, easily repeated. As the words repeat over and over, we reach the point of not even thinking about those words. Trappist Fr. M. Basil Pennington, the late contemplative prayer expert, says that this repetition lets the words of the prayer sink in until they penetrate — and form — the heart. Fr. Pennington noted:

> Orthodox monks are first taught to say the prayer out loud over and over again, in a soft voice, until it becomes repeated in the mind. Not unlike the way a tune catches in your head.[6]

But, unlike a silly tune going round and round in your mind to the point of distraction, the Jesus Prayer — and its cousin, the Rosary — serves as a focal point. By training our minds to, as Paul said, "pray constantly," we hope to become like that anonymous Russian peasant in *The Way of a Pilgrim*, who wrote:

> When I prayed in my heart, everything around me seemed delightful and marvelous.... The invocation of the Name of Jesus gladdened my way.[7]

In the Rosary, we also speak the name of Jesus. And doing so invokes upon us the same healing power of the Holy Name.

CHAPTER 5

Sacramentals: The Lamplight and the Power Plant

Quick — how many sacramentals did you use in the last few days?

Did you make a Sign of the Cross? Dip your fingers in the holy water font at church this week? Do you have a palm from last Passion Sunday stuck behind a holy picture at home? Is there a crucifix in your house? Do you own a holy medal?

How about that Rosary in your hand?

Each one is a sacramental.

Now there's a big difference between sacramentals and sacraments. It's like comparing a lamp with an electric plant. The lamp doesn't — and can't — do much without electricity. In the same way, sacramentals aren't much without the sacraments.

Sacramentals are inseparably linked with sacraments. Sacraments are the most important and totally necessary part of the connection. They are the liturgical actions through which we experience the power and love of God (grace) brought to us through the action of the Paschal Mystery (the Passion, death, and resurrection of Christ) and the working of the Holy Spirit.

Sacraments are necessary to our growth in Christian life. Sacramentals aren't. But sacramentals resemble sacraments and derive some power from those sacraments.

According to the Vatican II document on the liturgy:

[Sacramentals] signify effects, particularly of a spiritual kind, that are obtained through the Church's intercession. They dispose people to receive the chief effect of the sacraments and they make holy various occasions in human life.[8]

SACRAMENTS VERSUS SACRAMENTALS

Sacraments and sacramentals both involve grace, which makes things holy, but in different ways. Sacraments are divine in origin; they were instituted by Christ and impart grace directly through Christ himself as He celebrates these sacraments.

Sacramentals are instituted by the Church. (Today, according to canon law, the Apostolic See has the sole right to regulate sacramentals, create new ones, abolish old ones, and modify others as it sees a need.[9]) Sacramentals confer grace through the Church's power of intercession, a power granted to the Church by Christ. Sacramentals prepare us to receive grace and to cooperate with that grace working in our lives.

While there are only seven sacraments — a number that cannot change, as Christ himself instituted them — there are countless sacramentals. Sacraments mark the key moments of human life — baptism, marriage, death — and bring God's power and love into those moments.

The numbers of sacramentals are endless. Sacramentals address the countless times in our lives when we need to reach out for God's blessings, when we need to share in the energy that comes through the power of the prayer of the Church.

Canon law states:

> Sacramentals are sacred signs by which spiritual effects especially are signified and are obtained by the intercession of the Church.[10]

While sacramentals are linked to all the sacraments, many of the sacramentals have special links to at least one particular sacrament. For example, holy water is a sacramental that derives from the water used for baptism. (Not all holy water comes from a baptism, but the blessing of holy water is based upon the power of the waters of baptism.) Ashes are linked to the sacrament of reconciliation. And chalices and altar cloths are blessed by the presence of the holy species of bread and wine that touch them during the celebration of the Eucharist.

SACRAMENTALS: ACTIONS OR THINGS

In grouping the many types of sacramentals, we can do so in two major categories:

Actions — such as the Sign of the Cross, exorcisms, or the saying of the Divine Office (the daily prayer of the Church); and

Things — such as medals, scapulars, or holy water.

The Rosary falls somewhere in the middle. The beads of the Rosary are things and can be made from various objects including wood, ivory, metal, stone, or even olive pits or crushed rose petals. But the prayers said with the Rosary and its meditations upon the mysteries of Christ constitute actions.

Even though they lack the power of the sacraments, sacramentals do produce beneficial effects because they impart the grace that flows from the sacrament they represent. For example, sacramentals have the power to drive away evil spirits and to provide protection in times of temptation. While they do not remit venial sin, they can predispose a person to repentance and the action of grace. As the *Baltimore Catechism* reminded us, the use of sacramentals inspires us to great love of God and greater sorrow for our sins. This devotion, love, and sorrow open us to God's grace, and God's grace forgives venial sins.[11]

Also, sacramentals can be used to obtain temporal favors — as in the graces we hope will fall upon us via blessings of a new house or of seeds and spring fields before planting.

However, because of the link between sacraments and sacramentals, people can become confused, sometimes acting as if sacramentals had holy, even magical, powers on their own. A sacramental *does* have a quality of sacredness. However, its "power" comes from the power of the Church's prayer — with which the sacramental is blessed — and from the devotion and faith of the person using it in conjunction with that prayer of the Church. The proper use of a sacramental comes from linking one's own prayer with that of Christ's Mystical Body, the Church.

Sacramentals are best viewed as extensions of the liturgy in which all Christ's faithful people participate. Sacramentals can enhance both personal and community prayer. They also serve to remind us of the sacraments, and of God's loving presence and action in our daily lives.

As we count each bead of the Rosary, we can remember that many holy things touch us, slipping into our lives as easily as beads slip through our fingers, lighting up every moment with a little bit of God's powerful grace.

CHAPTER 6

The How, When, and Wear of the Rosary

Being able to keep a Rosary close at hand has always been part of the charm of rosaries. They fit nicely into a purse or a pocket. Auto rosaries hang within easy reach from rearview mirrors, or have a clip to attach them to the steering wheel. Ring rosaries fit neatly on the hand.

Religious men and women in traditional habit often have a Rosary attached to their rope belts. And, in Spanish cultures, couples are adorned with a double wedding Rosary (*el lazo*), often made of orange blossoms, as part of their marriage ceremony.

Even rock stars and teenagers wear rosaries — though more as a fashion statement than a sign of religious devotion.

But while there are several ways to wear a Rosary or keep it close at hand, there is generally only one way to pray it — at least in regards to the most common Dominican form of the Rosary. And its beads are the guide to its use.

HOW TO PRAY THE ROSARY

The Crucifix. As with all forms of Christian prayer, our focus is on Christ. Even with Marian devotions such as the Rosary, we follow the guidance of the Blessed Mother and her words in the Gospel of John: "Do whatever he tells you" (John 2:5). This is why the Rosary always begins with the Cross.

The Sign of the Cross. Many people will use the crucifix on their Rosary to bless themselves with the Sign of the Cross, touching the cross to their foreheads, chest, and shoulders. Many will kiss the cross as they make the sign that marks all Christians. The Cross sign reminds us of who we are and in whose image we are made — the Crucified and Risen One. It also places us in the presence of the Great Mystery, the divine Trinity: Father, Son, and Holy Spirit.

The Apostles' Creed. The Sign of the Cross is really the first prayer of the Rosary. Proceeding into the Rosary, the crucifix remains held in the hand as a focus for the next prayer, the Apostles' Creed. Traditionally attributed to the twelve apostles, the creed is actually a profession of faith that arose in the early Church. While under one hundred words, this is the longest of the Rosary's prayers and serves to remind us of our baptismal promises.

First Bead. On the first bead of the Rosary's pendant, we say the Lord's Prayer, the prayer given to us by Jesus himself when his followers asked him to teach them to pray (Luke 11:1 and Matthew 6:9–13). The prayer contains certain petitions (five in Luke and seven in Matthew) that, as St. Augustine (d. 430) said, contain everything for which we would ever need to ask.

The Next Three Beads. These beads are devoted to the Hail Mary, called the *Ave*, from its Latin first word. Here we begin to place ourselves beside Mary as we reflect in our hearts upon the mysteries of her Son's life.

The Second Single Bead. Here, the Glory Be (*Gloria Patri*) is said for the first time. This prayer is a form of a doxology, or "words of praise." It serves both to offer worship to God and remind us that the mysteries of our salvation were accomplished through the working of the Three Persons in One: the Father, Son, and Holy Spirit. Some people also add what is commonly known as the Fatima Decade Prayer after this bead, and after each Glory Be said in the Rosary, though this is an optional practice.

The Decades of the Rosary. As we enter the circle of the Rosary, we begin the five decades of beads, each set separated by four single beads. The circle of the Rosary reminds us of the encircling love of God and of the unending nature of our prayer in Christ. Each of the five decades of the Rosary focuses on five related mysteries of the life of Christ: the Joyful, Sorrowful, Glorious, and, since 2002, the Luminous Mysteries.

The Rosary Medallion. The series of each of the five mysteries begins with a knot, bead or medallion, often called the centerpiece, attached to the string holding the pendant of the first prayer beads and the crucifix. Depending on the type of Rosary being used, this medal can depict Mary, one of the saints, a mystery of the Lord's life (such as a chalice), or a representation of his life (such as the Infant of Prague). The series of mysteries is announced on the centerpiece of the Rosary.

FIVE AND TEN

The centerpiece medal acts as the first single bead of the five decades. On these main beads, each particular mystery is announced — such as "The First Joyful Mystery, the Annunciation" — and then, an Our Father is prayed. On each of the ten beads following, the Hail Mary is said, while one allows one's mind and heart to reflect upon the particular mystery. At the end of each decade, a Glory Be is prayed.

The *Salve Regina*. At the end of each set of five mysteries, after the last Glory Be, the *Salve Regina* — "Hail, Holy Queen" — is commonly prayed. This particular prayer is an antiphon, a hymn used during the daily prayer of the Church, the Liturgy of the Hours. The Marian antiphons, of which there are four, are said at Compline — the last prayer of the day, now better known as Night Prayer. The *Salve* antiphon is sung during Ordinary Time in the Church and reminds us of Mary's role in the life of Christ, whose ministry revealed the mercy of God at work in the world.

Nice, But Not Necessary. After the "*Salve Regina*," other prayers may be added to the Rosary. These often include a prayer to St. Michael, the *Memorare*, and/or a prayer to St. Joseph. However, these are not necessary to the completion of a full Rosary.

The End Is the Beginning. The Rosary is ended as it was begun, focused upon Christ, with the Sign of the Cross.

Each of these prayers of the Rosary has something to add to the meditations of its mysteries, and a deeper exploration of each prayer will be presented in subsequent chapters.

WHEN TO PRAY THE ROSARY

Praying any or all the decades of the Rosary is acceptable at any time. However, certain mysteries of the Rosary are linked to certain times of the year, and even to certain days of the week.

Monday and Saturday are now the days of the week when the Joyful Mysteries are given special focus. Traditionally, the days for the Joyful Mysteries were Monday and Thursday, but this was changed with the addition of the Luminous Mysteries, which are now prayed on Thursdays.

Tuesday and Friday (the day on which Christ died on the cross) are the days reserved for the Sorrowful Mysteries.

On Wednesday and Sunday, the Glorious Mysteries are the focus of reflection.

Every Sunday, no matter the time of the year, is the Lord's Day — a "little Easter" celebrated in every week when we remember the Resurrection. Therefore, the Glorious Mysteries are always appropriate on Sundays, no matter the liturgical season. However, during Advent, it has become a custom to remember the Joyful Mysteries of the Rosary on the Lord's Day.

During Lent, the Sorrowful Mysteries are meditated upon every day, except for Sunday, when we remember that we are destined to be vested in the glory that is now Our Lord's.

CHAPTER 7

The Christian's Secret Sign — The Sign of the Cross

While the Rosary is a prayer that often identifies one as a Catholic, it is not the most familiar prayer that marks someone as a Christian. Not even the Lord's Prayer does that.

No, the most identifying prayer for any Christian doesn't even need to be spoken at all. It can be purely physical.

The Sign of the Cross — whether you're Roman Catholic, a member of the Eastern Orthodox Church, Anglican, or Lutheran — marks you as a follower of Christ.

The Sign of the Cross begins our prayers, our Masses and services, our celebrations of the sacraments, our devotionals such as the Rosary, and is used in all our blessings. In fact, the Sign of the Cross is a prayer all by itself, a form of physical prayer.

Physical prayer involves the entire body and, when used often enough, doesn't even require thought. How many times has the Sign of the Cross been automatic for you? You're halfway through it before you even realize you've raised your hand to your forehead. After years of use, the gesture becomes so ingrained, happening when needed and serving to draw the thoughts along with it, that it places us in a state of prayer before we even realize it.

Before his first celebration of the Feast of the Triumph of the Holy Cross (September 14, 2005) as Bishop of Rome, Pope Benedict XVI called the Sign of the Cross "the fundamental act" of Christian prayer:

> Making the Sign of the Cross . . . means saying a visible and public "yes" to the One who died and rose for us, to God who

31

in the humility and weakness of his love is the Almighty, stronger than all the power and intelligence of the world.[12]

Use of the Sign of the Cross itself dates to at least the third century, when it served both as a prayer and a blessing. Early Christian writers such as Hippolytus of Rome (second century), St. Cyril of Jerusalem (fourth century), and St. Theodoret of Antioch (fifth century) all spoke about using the Sign of the Cross.

It was clear that it was used from earliest times in the formula for the sacrament of baptism, which, of course, comes from Christ and is found at the end of Matthew's Gospel. Written toward the latter part of the first Christian century, this Gospel places the words for this prayer on the Lord's lips: "... baptizing them in the name of the Father and of the Son and of the Holy Spirit" (Matthew 28:19).

The writings of the early Church fathers spoke of the prevalence of the Sign of the Cross in more than the sacraments, including many matters of common daily life: Tertullian (d. A.D. 220), a prolific writer about early Church life, said the Sign of the Cross was made at every daily task, from meals to taking a bath (*De Corona* [*The Chaplet*], 30). And Cyril of Jerusalem wrote in his *Catecheses*:

Be the Cross our seal made with boldness by our fingers on our brow, and on everything; over the bread we eat, and the cups we drink; in our comings in, and goings out; before our sleep, when we lie down and when we rise up; when we are on the way, and when we are still.[13]

While the Sign of the Cross has a long history in Christian life, it was not the first sign by which the early followers of Christ identified themselves to each other in public. In its first centuries the Church was persecuted, and Christians were often killed at the order of Roman authorities. Consequently, when Christians met in public, in trying to keep their identities hidden, they often identified themselves to each other by a secret gesture. While this could have been a cross, this symbol did not appear in the earliest artwork of the Church, at least not as often as other symbols that related to the Eucharist or the Good Shepherd.

THE FISH

Instead, it was likely that the earliest secret sign among Christians was the sign of the fish. A simple curve could be drawn on the ground with a walking stick by a Christian pilgrim meeting a stranger in a new town. If that stranger were another Christian and recognized the sign, they could add a lower curve to make the fish symbol, letting the traveler know he could move on in safety.

The fish monogram, or fish symbol, was one of the earliest emblems used to represent Christ. It can be found on the walls of Roman catacombs dating back to the third century. The fish reminded people of the miracles of Jesus — such as the multiplication of loaves and fish — and was used as part of the early meals shared in common (called the *agape* meals) that included the celebration of the Eucharist.

However, the fish symbol is also a play on words. Fish, in Greek, is ICHTHYS. If you use the first letters of the phrase "Jesus Christ, Son of God, Savior" — using the Greek words *Iesous Christos, Theou Hyios, Soter* — they becomes ΙΧΘΥΣ, or ICHTHYS in our alphabet. So the humble fish sketch, called a *rebus* or picture word, was also a primitive creed, because it allowed the one who drew it to express belief in Jesus's divinity and his role in salvation.

Like the fish symbol, the Sign of the Cross speaks without words, symbolizing much with a few simple gestures. The motions alone used to make the sign speak of God's own actions in Christ: coming down from heaven to become human upon earth, stretching himself out to give to others, to suffer and die, and then to pass through death and to rise up again. Our fingers trace this divine passage from our foreheads, down our chests and over our hearts, from one shoulder and passing to the next and ending in folded hands lifted up. Some in the Orthodox traditions even complete the Sign of the Cross by moving their right hand down to touch their right side, remembering the wounded side of Christ on the cross and the blood and water that flowed from it to give birth to the Church.

And yes, the right hand is used to make the Sign of the Cross.

Continuing to look at the Sign of the Cross without any reference to the words of the prayer, the very way in which we hold our fingers while making the sign contains still more lessons about the faith we are expressing. There are several ways to hold the fingers while making the Sign of the Cross, and each says something about the person of Jesus Christ:

- Using an open hand to make the sign, with all five fingers joined and upright, symbolizes the five wounds of Christ.
- Using the index and middle fingers held upright and tightly together, while curling the other two fingers over and touching the ring finger with the thumb, proclaims the two natures of Christ — both human and divine, united eternally in one person. The curled fingers also indicated the Trinity. This is the most common way to hold the fingers in the Western church.
- Using the index finger only, or the thumb, proclaims the oneness of God.
- Three fingers upright, or the index and middle finger with the thumb straight, or joined to the first two fingers, professes the Trinity.
- Found more commonly in the Eastern traditions is the practice of joining the tips of the first two fingers and the thumb together, as if holding a secret tightly in their grasp, while curling the other two fingers into the palm. This also signifies both the Trinity and the dual natures of Christ.
- In Spanish cultures, it is also common to kiss the thumb after making the Sign of the Cross. This is done with the thumb crossing the index finger, in a manner reminiscent of the cross, and can be considered to be a small veneration of that cross.

Whatever way we make the Sign of the Cross, with all its many meanings and symbols, we should think of this prayer the way Pope Benedict XVI described it when he visited the Shrine of Lourdes on its 150th anniversary in 2008. The pope reminded those gathered that Mary had begun her first apparition to St. Bernadette by making the Sign of the Cross:

The Sign of the Cross is a kind of synthesis of our faith, for it tells us how much God loves us; it tells us that there is a love in this world that is stronger than death, stronger than our weaknesses and sins. The power of love is stronger than the evil which threatens us.[14]

The Sign of the Cross

In the name of the Father,
and of the Son,
and of the Holy Spirit.
Amen.

CHAPTER 8

Which Apostle Wrote about the Virgin Birth? —
The Apostles' Creed

Following the opening prayer of the Rosary — the Sign of the Cross that needs no words — we move to the Apostles' Creed, which has many words. This longest prayer of the Rosary is usually said while still holding the crucifix of the Rosary.

According to long-standing tradition, the twelve apostles wrote the Apostles' Creed on the day of Pentecost, under the direction of the Holy Spirit, while gathered in prayer around the Blessed Virgin. Each of the Twelve contributed one statement of belief — one of the twelve articles of the faith — to that creed.

The Golden Legend, a European best-seller from the late thirteenth century, presented the Apostles' Creed as just such an instant creation: St. Peter, as prince of the apostles, was said to have written the first line: "We believe in God the Father almighty, creator of heaven and earth." Each apostle went on from there, until it fell to the newly appointed replacement of Judas Iscariot — Matthias — to conclude the listing of beliefs with "life everlasting."

While it is a wonderful legend and serves to emphasize the role of the apostles as teachers of the church, in reality, this creed, along with that other most familiar (and somewhat longer) creed — the Nicene-Constantinople Creed used at Sunday Mass — developed over time.

That's not to say there weren't creeds among the earliest disciples of Christ, and even among his apostles. A creed is a profession of faith, a statement of doctrinal beliefs — dating back to Mary Magdalene's statement on the first Easter: "I have seen the Lord"

(John 20:18). You could go back even earlier and say that Martha professed her faith in Jesus's power when she stood outside Lazarus's tomb and said, "Yes, Lord, I believe you are the Christ, the Son of God" (John 11:27). In fact, to call Jesus "Lord" or "Christ" was to profess belief in his divine nature, mission, and power.

Creeds are not limited to Christians. Twice a day, Jews profess their core belief by saying the *Shema:* "Hear O Israel, the Lord our Lord, the Lord is One." And Muslims pray the *Shahada* five times each day, proclaiming Allah as God and Mohammed as his messenger.

Even Mary's *Magnificat* (Luke 1:46–55) is a profession of faith in the greatness and mercy of God and echoes words from yet another mother graced by God: Hannah, the mother of Samuel, the first great prophet of ancient Israel (2 Samuel 2:1–10).

In early Christianity, creeds were short and simple statements, such as "Jesus is Lord." They were so short that they were originally called "symbols" — from a Greek word that meant "to put together," as in a contract. But symbol also meant what it does now, a sign or image, much as a cross is a symbol of the Christian faith. Two of the earliest creeds are believed to have been "put together" in Paul's first letters, to the Corinthians (1 Corinthians 15:3–8) and to the Romans (10:9).

"OLD ROMAN SYMBOL"

Since the Lord commanded his disciples to "baptize all nations" in the name of the Trinity — using the Sign of the Cross — the first formal developments of creeds can be found in baptismal promises. Early Christian baptisms included a form of an interrogation based on Christ's teachings and the faith taught by the apostles and handed on to believers. The "Old Roman Symbol" — a source of serious debate between Catholics and Protestants regarding early creeds — developed along these same lines, somewhere around the fifth century. The Symbol appears to have been used as a baptismal creed and included three parts of questions for candidates who had been prepared for baptism in the faith. Each part dealt with one person of the Trinity.

- The first part of the Symbol addressed belief in the First Person of the Trinity and the work of creation.
- The second part dealt with faith in Christ, his Incarnation, and his divine Paschal Mystery of redemption.
- The last part addressed the Holy Spirit and the work of sanctification, including the life of the Church.

What we now call the Apostles' Creed developed out of this formula of the Old Roman Symbol, or out of one very similar to it. The most ancient form of the Apostles' Creed could date as far back as the early third century. While it was not developed by the twelve apostles in a group, each of its twelve articles can be found in the New Testament. The *Catechism of the Catholic Church*, quoting St. Ambrose in the fourth century, says the Apostles' Creed faithfully summarizes the apostles' faith:

> [It was] the ancient baptismal symbol of the Church of Rome. Its great authority arises from this fact: it is "the Creed of the Roman Church, the See of Peter, the first of the apostles, to which he brought the common faith."
>
> — No. 194

Since it was developed so early, the Apostles' Creed was embraced by and is still used by almost all Christian denominations, including Lutherans, Anglicans, Episcopalians, Methodists, and some Baptists.

Within its three main parts, each dealing with a Person of the Trinity, the Apostles' Creed makes twelve points — called the "Articles of Faith." These express belief in God (1), and in the mission and Paschal Mystery of Christ (2–7), and the Holy Spirit at work in the Church (8–12):

1. I believe in God, the Father almighty, Creator of heaven and earth,
2. and in Jesus Christ, his only Son, our Lord,
3. who was conceived by the Holy Spirit, born of the Virgin Mary,
4. suffered under Pontius Pilate, was crucified, died and was buried;
5. he descended into hell; on the third day he rose again from the dead;
6. he ascended into heaven, and is seated at the right hand of God the Father almighty;
7. from there he will come to judge the living and the dead.
8. I believe in the Holy Spirit,
9. the holy catholic Church, the communion of saints,
10. the forgiveness of sins,
11. the resurrection of the body,
12. and life everlasting. Amen.

These articles of faith define the beliefs of the church, the Body of Christ. And this is why the church, described in article 9, is named with a lower case "c," since "catholic" means "universal." The Church of Christ is called to unite all believers into the one Body of Christ. These articles also unite us to each other in the Communion of Saints — those who have clung to these beliefs through centuries, right back to the twelve apostles.

There is another creed, the Nicene-Constantinople Creed, which is the one we pray at Mass on Sunday. It presents similar articles of belief but is a more complex profession of that faith. This creed developed a bit later than the Apostles' Creed, during times when the Church was dealing with various heresies centered around the understanding of Christ and of the Holy Spirit. This newer creed took shape in A.D. 325, at the Council of Nicaea, and was further developed by the Council of Constantinople in A.D. 381. It reached its present form by A.D. 451, when the Council of Chalcedon ordered its use for the entire Church. It is professed by the Eastern Church as well the Western — although a major disagreement over the statement about the Holy Spirit "proceeding from the Father and the Son" developed and played a role in the Great Schism of 1054, which split the Eastern Orthodox from the Western Church.

These two creeds are joined by a few lesser-known others, such as the Athanasian Creed (called the *Quicumque vult* — "Whosoever wishes to be saved" — dating to the sixth century, but traditionally ascribed to St. Athanasius, the fourth-century Bishop of Alexandria) and the *Credo of the People of God* (proclaimed by Pope Paul VI in 1968). But all creeds serve the same purpose. They "call to mind and confess the great mysteries of the faith,"[15] both in daily prayer and during the celebration of the great mysteries of our faith — especially at baptism and the Eucharist.

SO WHO WROTE THE APOSTLES' CREED?

Answer: None of the apostles — at least not directly. On that first Pentecost, John didn't sit down and write that Jesus was God's son. His brother, James, didn't snatch the pen away to scribble something about the Virgin Birth. Instead, all of these beliefs were written out over the course of many years.

However, the apostles, and the rest of Jesus's first disciples, did believe all the basics of what was later written down in the creeds. And they taught those beliefs to those who followed after them. And that was passed on to all of us who follow in the path of the apostles today, still saying *Credo* ("I believe") to everything that we recite in this prayer until we reach the very end and firmly say, "Amen."

CHAPTER 9

Getting Back to Basics on a Two-Way Street — *The Lord's Prayer*

The Rosary, as already noted, began as a knotted cord used for saying 150 Lord's Prayers as a substitute for the monastic tradition of praying the 150 psalms each day.

At the beginning of the Way of the Cross in Jerusalem, on the Mount of Olives — right across from the Church of the Ascension — is Pater Noster (Latin for "Our Father") Church. It is a nineteenth-century church built, as many in the Holy City are, on the ruins of an older church. This one is said to date to the time of St. Helen (d. 330), the mother of the Roman Emperor Constantine, who ordered churches to be built on many of the holy sites related to the life of Jesus Christ.

Pater Noster Church has a baptistery whose walls are lined with mosaics of the Lord's Prayer written in sixty-two languages, including Aramaic, the language Jesus spoke. Various linguistics sites on the Internet cite hundreds more translations of this prayer, which is found in two Gospels: Matthew 6:9–13 and Luke 11:1–13. (A third version appears in the second-century writing known as the *Didache*, or "The Teachings of the Twelve Apostles," which directed people to pray three times a day. The *Didache* was considered to be lost for centuries, but was rediscovered in 1873 in a monastery in Turkey.)

Mathew's version of the Lord's Prayer has Jesus teaching the prayer during the Sermon on the Mount. It is presented within the context of prayer, fasting, and giving alms. (The *Didache* also places the prayer within its teaching about fasting.) In Luke's Gospel, the context of instruction comes during Jesus's own prayer life, when one of the disciples asks the Lord to "teach us to pray" (Luke 11:1).

Under Pater Noster Church lies a series of caves. Tradition says that it was here that Jesus taught this prayer, no doubt following the wording of Luke's Gospel. Whether this is the case or not, the caves nonetheless give a sense of quiet and peace that would be reminiscent of a place where Jesus might have withdrawn to pray.

While Luke's Gospel was written after Matthew's, many Bible scholars believe Luke's version of the Pater Noster — being shorter and simpler — is closest to what Jesus originally said. However, it is Matthew's version that is more familiar to us today. It is this Matthean version of the Lord's Prayer that starts each decade of the Rosary.

The Lord's Prayer is simple, less than sixty words — so basic that the Church, from earliest times, required it to be recited by baptismal candidates or their sponsors (once infant baptism rose in popularity). Matthew's version contains seven parts, or petitions (Luke's has five). Yet these petitions, as St. Augustine wrote in the fourth century, cover everything we would ever need to ask for in prayer. And Tertullian, a prolific third-century Christian apologist, called the prayer "the epitome of the whole gospel."

PETITIONS OF THE LORD'S PRAYER

The prayer's purpose is simple — worshiping God and asking for basic daily needs. Its petitions can be broken into two groups: first dealing with God and then with us.

First, God.

What could be more central? God is creator of all things and the goal of our existence. As the Psalmist said, "Take away their breath and they perish" (Psalm 104). Without God, none of the other basics really matters.

So the Lord's Prayer first acknowledges God's centrality.

• *Our Father, Who Art in Heaven.* This introductory phrase addresses God both intimately — as a child speaks to a beloved parent — as well as from an awe-filled distance (since God exists "in heaven" — a state of perfection, peace, and glory that we cannot yet know). However, by having us call God "Our Father," we also remember, as does the *Catechism of the Catholic Church*, that heaven is the "homeland toward which we are heading and to which, already, we belong" (No. 2802).

We want to get home — where we belong — and to be closer to God. The next three petitions specifically express this desire to be in God's presence:

• *Hallowed Be Thy Name.* To hallow a name is to honor it, to acknowledge its holiness. The word "hallow" comes from the same old European roots that give us the word "holy" and which ultimately signify wholeness and perfection.

Additionally, in the ancient world, to know a person's name was to be intimate with him or her. Names were not given freely to a stranger, but only shared with close associates, friends and family. Today, in many Eastern cultures, this remains true. People are referred to by their place in a family — such as "youngest sister" or "mother's second brother" — rather than by their real names. So when we "hallow" God's name, we are saying we want to draw closer to God, to be closer to knowing God's "real name," just as we know that God — through Jesus — has drawn close to us.

• *Thy Kingdom Come* is also a petition seeking God's nearness and expressing our longing to dwell in the presence of God that is called "the Kingdom." Jesus himself proclaimed that Kingdom — where freedom, love, and health belong to all.

• *Thy Will Be Done on Earth as It Is in Heaven.* Yet again, we express our longing for God and the ways of God's Kingdom. By speaking these words, we place ourselves at God's disposal, asking God to direct us according to his plan, his will. We express a desire to be part of making God's will present not only in heaven but on earth. In this way, we echo Mary, when she told the angel, "May it be done to me according to your word" (Luke 1:38), as well as Jesus when he submitted himself to God's will in Gethsemane.

In this petition, both longing and action are linked. Our prayers must always dispose us to action, to first approach God in prayer and then be willing to act — as Mary and Jesus were — in whatever way God asks. In that way, our petitions may become reality — if

God's grace is given to us. We have our part in making the Kingdom come — and it doesn't just involve praying about it. As St. Thomas Aquinas said, speaking about this petition of the Lord's Prayer, it reveals that "two things are necessary for eternal life: the grace of God and the will of man."[16]

In this way, we begin to see how the Lord's Prayer is a two-way street. We approach God and seek to do his will, but then we ask God to approach us and to act in our own world. The first three petitions of the Lord's Prayer have sometimes been called the "You petitions," since they move our thoughts toward God. However, since the Lord's Prayer is a two-way street that links our actions and God's grace, once we have asked to be drawn closer to God in the heavenly kingdom, we then ask God to draw near to us in our world of daily needs.

The next four petitions of the Lord's Prayer can thus be called the "Us petitions." They bring us back from thoughts of heaven to dealing with the needs of earth: our physical and emotional well-being, as well as that of the world around us.

Here, as in the first petitions, we must always remember that none of these is a private petition — the Lord's Prayer is not about me and God, but about us and God; that it why we were taught to say: "Our Father."

• *Give Us This Day Our Daily Bread.* Nothing is more basic than food. Without it, we die. So this petition deals with pure physical survival. (Yes, there is the reminder in Matthew 4:4 that we do not live on bread alone. But that also deals with temptation and the need for spiritual strength, which are addressed a little later in this prayer. For now, we are dealing with pure physical need.)

God knows, of course, that we need to eat. We really don't need to tell him that. However, we need to remember that "all good things come from God," as St. Teresa of Ávila said. The request for daily bread reminds us that God provided manna in the desert — but only enough for one day, anything kept longer than that spoiled — and that God continues to feed us, in various ways, in just the right amount. We must remember to trust that, like the lilies of the field, God will provide for our needs.

• *Forgive Us Our Trespasses as We Forgive Those Who Trespass against Us.* The Lord's Prayer is definitely a two-way street: we give God honor and worship, and we ask God, in return, to give us what we need. This petition illustrates this two-way street concept again, this time in the area of physical relationships. We ask for God's mercy — an unending need. But, as we pray those words, we are, at the same time, asking forgiveness for others, since we say "our trespasses" and not "my trespasses." In fact, as we ask for mercy, we are also promising to extend mercy to those who sin against us. We say "as we forgive," not "after we forgive," or "and then we will forgive."

After voicing these two petitions — and trusting that, through God's grace, we will be in a healthy, well-fed relationship with God and others — we have to remember that we probably won't stay there. We will continue to need help. Again and again.

So we pray for the future.

• *Lead Us Not into Temptation.* First of all, God doesn't tempt anyone (see James 1:11). That task is the venue of someone else in the story of salvation. This "temptation" translation of the verse comes from older Latin versions of the Lord's Prayer as they rendered verse thirteen in Matthew's sixth chapter. The current translation reads, "Do not subject us to the final test."

In Greek, the first written language of the New Testament, the word that we see as "temptation" is *peirasmos*. This is one of those words that has several meanings, one of which can be "temptation." But *peirasmos* can also mean "trial," "adversity," or "a test in character." It can also refer to an ultimate type of test, such as a "final judgment." However, whatever *peirasmos* refers to, it should definitely serve to remind us that we are all tested, throughout life. Since we have hearts susceptible to both trial and temptation, we can easily move away from God's presence. So, in our prayer, we ask to avoid anything that would draw us away from

God, tempting us to follow the way of the world rather than the way of the Kingdom.

• *Deliver Us from Evil.* There is definitely evil in the world. None of us escapes its touch. The *Catechism of the Catholic Church* teaches that this part of the Lord's Prayer "brings before the Father all the distress of the world" (No. 2854).

Often, we are like children huddled in the dark and cold. Yet we know that the dark has been scattered by the Light of Christ, who has overcome the world and the cold of death and sin. When we are close to God, we can more easily see that freeing light, even in the darkest moments.

• Finally, as we say *Amen* — which means "I believe" — we express our willingness to accept that the delivering Light of Christ reveals for us the Father's glory and leads us into the Kingdom, both on earth and in heaven.

Seven petitions. The Lord covered a lot with a few words: light overcomes darkness; bread overcomes hunger; love heals, and forgiveness mends; good banishes evil.

So, if we sincerely pray the prayer that the Lord taught us, we will feel ourselves to be in the presence of the love of God. Here, right in the midst of our daily hunger, darkness, and need for forgiveness. God With Us is still with us, still helping us pray. Jesus, God made flesh, knew about the here and now of our needs, and about how God — here and now — is ready to answer us and draw us into his kingdom.

The Lord's Prayer (*Our Father*)

Our Father, who art in heaven,
hallowed be thy name;
thy kingdom come;
thy will be done
on earth as it is in heaven.
Give us this day our daily bread;

and forgive us our trespasses
as we forgive those
who trespass against us;
and lead us not into temptation,
but deliver us from evil.
Amen.

CHAPTER 10

The Hail Mary in Three Acts

Greetings and salutations!
It may sound old-fashioned, but this medieval greeting is basically what the angel Gabriel offered to Mary at the Annunciation. He greeted her and wished her well, saluting her as favored by God and with God. All in a few words: "Greetings, favored one! The Lord is with you" (cf. Luke 1:28).

The "Hail Mary" is the centerpiece of the Rosary. And it all begins with a greeting.

In fact, each of the three parts of this prayer contains a greeting, offered by different individuals, to the Mother of God.

However, this most famous Marian prayer was not truly even a prayer as it was first used.

The "Hail Mary" is about the life of Mary, the Blessed Virgin and Holy Mother. Parts of the prayer date to the earliest days of the Church and can be found in the Gospel of Luke. The Latin translation of this Gospel — done as early as the second century but revised most famously by St. Jerome in A.D. 382, from Greek texts — even gives us the first of three names by which this prayer is known:

The *Ave*. The Hail Mary is sometimes called by this name because it begins with the Latin word for "hail" or "greetings." *Ave* offers, in one word, what can be found in each of the three parts of the prayer: greetings, recognition, and honor. *Ave* to the Romans was a royal salute, given to Caesar. So it was a natural for the early Church, as it developed in a Roman culture, to offer this greeting to Christ's mother.

The Angelic Salutation. The Hail Mary is less commonly known by this title, which refers to the first words said by Gabriel to Mary in the Gospel of Luke. In the original Greek of the Gospel writers, the words spoken by the angel are "*Chaire, kechairetomene.*" These words, which we know as "Hail, full of grace" better translate as "Be well, highly favored one." They show both Gabriel's concern that Mary not be afraid, and his reassurance that she is chosen by God.

The Hail Mary. This best-known title for the prayer is the English translation of the Latin *Ave Maria*, the prayer's first words in Latin.

Whatever you choose to call this most beloved of Marian prayers, it consists of three distinct parts: the first two coming from Scripture and the third added by the Church, following the lead of popular piety. Each part of the Hail Mary is like an act in a play, with distinct roles for those pronouncing the words that became our familiar prayer.

ACT ONE: THE ANGELIC GREETING

Here, in the first scene, the words go to the angel. In Luke's Gospel, Gabriel speaks to Mary and his first words are, noted above, well wishes and an announcement of God's love and favor. In the prayer, these are presented as "Hail (Mary), full of grace, the Lord is with you." The prayer adds Mary's name to the Gospel greeting (Luke 1:28), a practice that developed later and can be confirmed back to at least the eleventh century.

Gabriel's words also echo a prophecy of Zechariah: "Sing and rejoice, O daughter Zion! See, I am coming to dwell among you, says the LORD" (Zechariah 2:14). The promise of God spoken by the prophet Zechariah ariah was for a people living in exile who were about to return to rebuild the Lord's temple. The prophecy promised God's salvation to the people of Israel, just as Gabriel's words promised salvation to all people because of God's holy presence in Jesus Christ.

Still on the note of Mary's role in salvation history, the Eastern churches (both Orthodox and Byzantine) use a prayer similar to the Hail Mary, but theirs begins "*Theotokos*, Virgin, rejoice. Mary, full of grace…" *Theotokos*, which means "God-bearer" in Greek, acknowledges this woman as, first of all, the Mother of God and then as virgin. Only after acknowledging her exalted status does the prayer move to announcing Mary's given name.

It is interesting to note that the original Greek versions of the Gospels do not credit Gabriel with calling Mary "full of grace." That title came with the Latin translation, several centuries later. The Greek term *plaras karitos* for "full of grace" does, however, appear in John's Gospel — just not used in reference to Mary. Rather the term speaks of Jesus (John 1:14). It also occurs in one other place, the Acts of the Apostles, where it refers to the deacon, Stephen, the first martyr (Acts 6:8).

ACT TWO: ELIZABETH'S GREETING

"Blessed are you among women and blessed is the fruit of your womb." Now the words of the play go to Mary's cousin, Elizabeth (Luke 2:42). Inspired by the Holy Spirit, she greets both Mary and Jesus when they arrive at her door. Elizabeth's words go on to honor Mary in her role as the Mother of God: "Who am I that the mother of my Lord should come to me?"

These two greetings compose the earliest part of the Hail Mary prayer. The early Church used them as a greeting honoring both Mary and Jesus — whose names were later added to the Gospel greetings. (Pope Urban IV is often credited with inserting the name of Jesus into the prayer in 1261. The Franciscan St. Bernardine of Siena, who had a devotion to the Holy Name of Jesus, is said to be the person who helped make this popular throughout Italy in the fifteenth century.)

The two greetings were the only parts of the Hail Mary prayer for centuries. They were said, together, in various Church settings, often in penitential situations, over the next 1,500 years. The Hail Mary greetings were often said with genuflections or prostrations — as many as 150 times in a row. (This paralleled the use of the 150 psalms in daily prayer and the use of 150 Lord's Prayers, and no doubt figured in the development of the Rosary itself.)

ACT THREE: THE ENDING PETITION
AND A CAST OF THOUSANDS

As it first existed, the Hail Mary was not a complete prayer, since it did not include a petition. True prayers contain four parts: praise offered to God, repentance, petition, and thanksgiving. Even the short "Glory Be," while perhaps not a complete prayer, includes a petition that God's glory continue forever.

This became a major criticism of the *Ave* by Protestant reformers in the sixteenth century. As it existed until then, the *Ave* only met the criteria of "praise" — since it acknowledged the Incarnation — and "repentance," given its use in penitential situations. It might even have been said to contain a "thanksgiving" phrase in that it acknowledged God's presence: "The Lord is with you." However, God, through the intercession of his Mother, was not asked for anything, thus leaving out the element of "petition." True prayer contains petitions, acknowledging that all good comes from God and that we need God's grace at all times.

The petition part of the *Ave* — "Holy Mary, Mother of God, pray for us sinners, now and at the hour of our death" — was formally added to the Breviary (the Church's book of daily prayers) in 1568, following the order of the Council of Trent in 1563. And here, the words — continuing with our analogy of a play — belong to us. We ask God, through the intercession of his mother, for blessings, grace, and forgiveness throughout our lives, up to the last moment of earthly life.

Various parts of this closing petition, of course, are far more ancient than the sixteenth century. As we have seen, "Mother of God" is a title the Church has given Mary since its earliest days. It was the Council of Ephesus, in A.D. 431, that declared Mary to be the Mother of God — the *Theotokos* (God-bearer) of the Eastern Church. Other translations of the *Ave* prayer, from across Europe and dating back many centuries, show that it was common in popular piety to add a petition seeking Mary's help for both sinners and the dying. It was the people themselves, working in their everyday lives, who probably first added the petition aspect to this prayer. Long before Trent, and certainly by 1514, the Liturgy of the Hours — the daily prayer of the Church, prayed most often in convents and monasteries, but the property and right of all Christians — contained an *Ave* with this now-familiar ending petition.

ONE FINAL NOTE ABOUT THE HAIL MARY

While the Hail Mary is the most famous of the Marian prayers, it is really a Christ-centered prayer. All true Christian prayer is Christ-centered. Each of the *Ave*'s three parts is intended to do what Mary did for Elizabeth — bring Christ to us. And we must do what Elizabeth did: come to know and draw close to Jesus through his mother. Whenever we turn to Mary, we must remember Jesus, who is always with her:

- When we greet Mary, we do so as the one to whom the Lord is present in a unique way, just as Gabriel said.
- When we acknowledge Mary as the blessed Mother of the Lord, we acknowledge the mystery of the Incarnation.
- Finally, we ask the Mother of God to intercede for us to her Son, just as she prayed at his cross at the hour of *his* death.

The *Catechism of the Catholic Church* says that the Hail Mary, like all Marian prayers, honors Christ by centering on the mysteries of his life (No. 2675). Mary witnessed these mysteries: his Incarnation and birth, his miracles, his ministry, his death, and his resurrection, as well as the sending of his Spirit upon the Church. It is fitting that we approach the Lord by greeting and saluting his mother, while seeking her guidance and assistance — just as Elizabeth, and all who came after her, did.

Hail Mary

Hail Mary, full of grace.

The Lord is with thee.
Blessed art thou among women,
and blessed is the fruit of thy womb, Jesus.
Holy Mary, Mother of God,
pray for us sinners,
now and at the hour of our death.
Amen.

Ave Maria (Hail Mary)

Ave Maria, gratia plena,
Dominus tecum.
Benedicta tu in mulieribus,
et benedictus fructus ventris tui, Iesus.

Sancta Maria, Mater Dei,
ora pro nobis peccatoribus,
nunc, et in hora mortis nostrae.
Amen.

CHAPTER 11

The Glory Be's Words of Praise

Just as every prayer — to be properly called "a prayer" — must contain an element of praise, so does the Rosary contain elements of praise. This is especially true at the end of each decade, which uses the prayer known as "the Glory Be." Its Latin name is the *Gloria Patri*, and it is properly called the Lesser Doxology.

"Doxology" comes from two Greek words: *doxa*, meaning "praise" or "glory," and *logos*, from the root for "word."

"Glory be to the Father and to the Son and to the Holy Spirit." Simple words of praise.

There is also a Great Doxology — the *Gloria* we say at Mass. Though it has more words, it is similar in purpose to the Lesser Doxology.

Doxologies, in many forms, predate the early Church. The first are found in Hebrew Scriptures and refer to God, the Creator. They are found at the end of each of the five books of the Psalms. For example, the doxology "Blessed be the Lord, the God of Israel, from all eternity and forever. Amen. Amen," concludes Psalm 41, at the end of the first book of Psalms. Another early doxology can be found in the Book of Exodus, where Moses's father-in-law, Jethro, praises God's power (Ex 18:10). Hymns of praise were also a common part of Jewish Temple worship in ancient Israel.

Scriptural doxologies became more numerous in the New Testament and include Mary's *Magnificat* (Luke 1:46–56), Simeon's canticle (Luke 2:14), and many parts of the letters of Paul (e.g. Romans 8:38–39). They are also found in the Book of Revelation. (See Revelation 4:8 and the praise of the four living creatures with six wings.)

In our liturgies, the Glory Be (Lesser Doxology) is not used as often as the Great Doxology — the *Gloria*, which is sometimes called the Angelic Hymn. That name comes from its first and most ancient lines — "Glory to God in the highest" — found in the infancy narratives of Luke's Gospel (Luke 2:14), the song of the angels at Christ's birth.

The *Gloria*, like the Glory Be, is essentially a joyous hymn and, therefore, is not used during Lent or Advent — except on special feasts, such as the Annunciation (March 25) and the feast of the Immaculate Conception (December 8).

The *Gloria's* first part, praising God alone, has been used since at least the second century. The later parts, dealing with Christ and the Spirit, were added around the fourth century. This was the time of several heresies about Christ, including the Arian heresy, which claimed that Jesus was not God but a creature of God who had been given divine powers after the Resurrection.

Part of the Church's response to the Arian heresy and other heresies like it was to cite prayers already in use — such as the *Gloria* — and expand on these existing doxologies to stress its teachings about the Trinity. Thus we came to have the words of what today is called the Eucharistic Doxology (or *Per Ipsum*): "Through him, and with him, and in him, O God, almighty Father, in the unity of the Holy Spirit, all glory and honor is yours, for ever and ever." A similar doxology at the end the Eucharistic prayer dates from the fifth century.

The Lesser or Minor Doxology, the *Gloria Patri*, was developed for a similar reason. The earliest forms of this prayer speak of giving glory to the Father "through Jesus Christ" and "in the Holy Spirit." However, because of theological controversy over the relationship of the Persons of the Trinity to each other, more words were added, since "through" and "in" might imply some subordination of the Second and Third Persons of the Trinity.

Controversy over how to address the first two Persons of the Trinity — regarding the relationship between the Father and the Son — was addressed by the Council of Nicaea (A.D. 325), which gave us the essentials of the Creed we now say at Sunday Mass.

The Council of Constantinople (A.D. 381) addressed the role of the Holy Spirit and gave us the final version of the same prayer, now formally called the Nicene-Constantinople Creed. It was approved for universal Church use in A.D. 451 by the Council of Chalcedon.

There is yet one more doxology said at the Mass. It comes after the Lord's Prayer: "For the kingdom, the power, and the glory are yours, now and for ever."

Part of this particular Lord's Prayer doxology can be dated to the ancient Church and is found in the second century in the *Didache*. However, the Lord's Prayer doxology we know today — though bearing a resemblance to the *Didache* version, "For the power and the glory are yours forever and ever" — comes from a parenthetical addition, called an embolism, to the Gospel of Matthew, added by a medieval transcriber of the Gospel. (Remember that the *Didache* was considered lost for centuries and only rediscovered in 1873, so its Lord's Prayer doxology was not available to this medieval scribe.)

While the *Gloria* we know today has been part of the Mass since the Fourth Synod of Toledo in A.D. 633, the Lesser Doxology, the Glory Be, is only used for Masses for children. Instead, its most common use is in the Rosary and the Liturgy of the Hours, the daily prayer of the Church. It is also used by Methodists, Lutherans, and Anglicans when reciting the Psalms and various forms of daily prayer. In the Eastern Church and the Orthodox churches, it is used for the Divine Liturgy (the Mass) and for private prayer.

However, whatever its form or history, a doxology's main purpose is to praise God and give honor to God's glory. And, no matter how beautiful the prayer, words are always a poor vehicle of expression.

So how can one best express proper praise for God's glory?

Jesus, "the image of the invisible God" (Colossians 1:15), gives us the example because he did this every day of his life on earth. His teachings, prayers, ministry, and miracles all gave praise to God. Therefore, his daily life could be called a doxology, a life lived in praise. This is why the meditations of the Rosary are also forms of doxologies, since they draw the mind and heart toward the glory of God, as revealed in the life of Christ, and inspire us to give praise, as Jesus taught us to do.

The Glory Be *(Gloria Patri)*

Glory be to the Father,
and to the Son,
and to the Holy Spirit.

As it was in the beginning,
is now, and ever shall be,
world without end.
Amen.

CHAPTER 12

War and Peace:
The *Salve Regina*

Prayers become favorites for many reasons. The *Gloria* is common for major celebrations, the Lord's Prayer for the beginning of the day, and the Twenty-third Psalm for the end of earthly life.

The *Salve Regina* (Latin for "Hail, Holy Queen") is a prayer that has often been used for protection — both when facing an enemy and at times of peace, for anything from someone seeking a safe night of sleep to crusaders marching on the Holy Land.

The *Salve Regina* is one of the four great Marian antiphons — sung during the daily prayer of the Church (the Liturgy of the Hours) at various times of the year, to honor the Mother of God. It is found in the Breviary. The four Marian antiphons are:

- *Salve Regina*, sung from Trinity Sunday until Advent.
- *Alma Redemptoris Mater* (Loving Mother of our Redeemer), sung during Advent and Christmas seasons.
- *Ave Regina Caelorum* (Hail, Queen of Heaven), sung from the Feast of the Presentation (February 2) through Good Friday.
- *Regina Caeli* (Queen of Heaven), with its many Alleluias "for He whom you did merit to bear," reserved for the season of the greatest feast of all: Easter.

The Marian antiphons are sung at Compline, or Night Prayer, as it is more commonly known today, which is the final prayer of the day in the Liturgy of the Hours. Compline is sung before retiring at night and seeks the blessings of peace throughout the night. It is meant to bring a sense of calm and reliance upon the mercy of the Lord. In monasteries and convents, Night Prayer often marks the start of the Great Silence, which continues through the night until Morning Prayer and Mass.

The *Salve* is often linked with religious communities. In fact, the Dominican order has used the antiphon since its earliest days in the thirteenth century and is often credited with placing this antiphon at the end of Night Prayer.

Like all antiphons, the *Salve* is a form of responsorial song that is paired with the chanting of psalms. However, unlike most other antiphons, the *Salve Regina* became popular in its own right, apart from its monastic use at daily prayer. It even became an anthem, sung by workmen in various guilds throughout Europe during the Middle Ages and by sailors on watch at sea during the night.

There are legends that tie the origin of the *Salve* to St. Anselm (d. 1080) or St. Bernard of Clairvaux (d. 1153). Others attribute the antiphon to Adhemar, Bishop of Podium (Puy-en-Velay) in France. Adhemar was the spiritual leader of the First Crusade, launched in 1096 by Pope Urban II. Because of Adhemar, who is said to have composed the antiphon as a warriors' song to seek the intercession of the Queen of Heaven, the antiphon is sometimes called the "Anthem of Le Puy." (Adhemar made the journey to Jerusalem, but died there in 1098.) However, today many scholars attribute this Marian anthem not to Adhemar but to Hermann Contractus (d. 1013), a German mathematician and poet.

Many years after that first crusade, another pope also felt that this anthem might benefit another earthly kingdom — that of the Papal States. In the mid-nineteenth century, Italy was beginning to coalesce into a single sovereign nation, instead of the many independent states that had existed for centuries before. In 1861, the Kingdom of Italy was formed, taking over land that had belonged to the Papal States. (The existence of the Papal States formally ended with the 1929 Lateran Treaty, which ceded the remaining papal lands in Italy to King Victor Emmanuel III in return for the establishment of the Vatican City-State as an independent nation.)

While the turmoil preceding the 1861 founding of the Kingdom of Italy was underway, Pope Pius IX asked that special prayers for the Papal States be added after Masses celebrated around the world. These prayers included three *Aves* and the *Salve Regina*.

While Pius did not require these prayers be said, a later pope did. Pope Leo XIII ordered these prayers to be said following Masses in the entire Church. The Leonine Prayers, as they came to be called, included the three *Aves*, the *Salve*, and the Prayer to St. Michael, and Pope Pius X added a triple invocation to the Sacred Heart of Jesus. The Leonine Prayers were said after each Low Mass, offered at the foot of the altar, until they were officially suppressed in 1965.

The "Low Mass" was the less formal version of the traditional Latin Mass, now called the "Extraordinary Form of the Roman Rite." It was usually celebrated on weekdays, with the "High Mass" cele-brated on Sundays and certain feast days. The High Mass was sung — all parts of the Mass — and often took two hours or more to celebrate, whereas a Low Mass could be completed in fifteen to twenty minutes.

Today, the *Salve Regina* remains a part of Night Prayer and the recitation of the Rosary. It is also a prayer near to the heart of many priests and is often a part of their funerals, sung by other priests in attendance. After Pope John Paul II was buried on April 8, 2005, the *Salve Regina* was sung by the priests who had gathered around his grave for his burial under St. Peter's Basilica.

Hail, Holy Queen *(Salve Regina)*

Hail, holy Queen, Mother of Mercy.
Hail, our life, our sweetness and our hope.
To you do we cry, poor banished children of Eve.
To you do we send up our sighs, mourning and weeping in
   this valley of tears.
Turn, then, most gracious advocate, your eyes of mercy
   toward us;
   and after this, our exile, show unto us the blessed fruit of
   your womb, Jesus.
O clement, O loving, O sweet Virgin Mary.
V. Pray for us, O holy Mother of God.
R. That we may be made worthy of the promises of Christ.

CHAPTER 13

"Sincerely Yours"...The Amen

That's it. Final. End of discussion.

We say it automatically, almost without thinking. "Amen." It's just how we end a prayer: "Amen."

In a way, the Amen is sort of like the end of a letter, the part just before our signature: the "sincerely yours" in "Sincerely yours, Jane Doe." It's an automatic and polite way to wrap things up.

All the prayers said in the Rosary end with an "Amen."

But "Amen" — as a word and as a religious statement — is more than just the end of a prayer, and it goes back much further than any of the prayers of the Rosary.

In fact, "Amen" is one of "those words" — one of the few words to make it from ancient Hebrew, unchanged, into all the Biblical translations. It began as "Amen" and it remains as "Amen" to this day. (Another word that made it through all of biblical history is found often in the New Testament: "alleluia.") For example, "Amen" appears in the Old Testament Book of Deuteronomy (27:14), which dates to the time of Moses (about 1450 B.C.), as well as toward the end of the Book of Revelation (22:20), written about 1,600 years later. (And even while Revelation was first written in Greek, the Hebrew "Amen" stayed in its original Hebrew in that Greek text.)

Over the centuries, while there have been other words used as substitutes — such as "truly" or "verily" — nothing has seemed to fit the bill as well as the original "Amen."

"Amen" is also one of "those words" that, in the sense of liturgy and worship, have multiple meanings. Another is "Eucharist," which means "thanksgiving" in its original Greek (*eucharisteō*), but also refers to the celebration of the Lord's Supper, the Mass, the sacrament of Holy Communion, and the sacred bread and wine that feed us.

So what multiple meanings do we express when we say "Amen"?

Amen in Hebrew comes from an even more ancient word, *'aman*, which means a variety of things dealing with certainty and truth: "faithful," "confirmed," "to be firm," and even "certainly." Loosely, *'aman* can mean the act of saying yes, though it is not to be seen simply as an affirmative statement because it involves more of the entire self in that confirming action. One of "amen's" roots also refers to security, as in something given in the form of a deposit.

For ancient Hebrews, the Amen was used as a type of adverb, to support an action or profession of faith. So when Moses listed the curses in Deuteronomy, the people answered, "Amen," meaning they accepted and agreed to the action of condemnation. The Amen was used to confirm and finalize both curses and blessings. It was also used, much as we do today, to end prayers. Prayers, that is, in the synagogue, but not in the Temple, if most sources are to be believed. This is because the Amen is a response of the faithful, of the congregation, and not of the person pronouncing the blessings or prayers — as the priests did inside the Temple, without the people present.

While the Amen was commonly used in prayer by the ancient Hebrews, it only appears about twenty to thirty times in the Old Testament. However, it appears over 100 times in the New Testament, and often on the lips of Jesus.

JESUS AND "AMEN"

We just noted that the Amen was spoken by those who heard a blessing, like a congregation in church, but not by the one conferring that blessing, such as a priest. Yet Jesus — whom Paul called our High Priest (see the letter to the Hebrews) — used it, and often. Why?

It seems that Jesus's usage of the Amen was different than the ancient Hebrew usage. He didn't use the Amen at the end of a statement or a prayer. (Not even in the Lord's Prayer, since the Amen there is at the end of a later addition — a doxology — to the prayer:

"For the kingdom, the power and the glory are yours, now and for-ever, Amen.") Instead, Jesus used the Amen as a beginning: "Amen, I say to you." (Sometimes we translate that as "truly or "verily".)

What was Jesus doing — bringing the ending to the beginning? Well, just as the Amen means many things, so Jesus was using it to say several things:

First, he was saying, "This is truth."

Next, he was telling his disciples to "believe this."

And, since belief brings action, he was also saying, "Act on this."

Finally, Jesus was speaking on his own divine authority. In the book of Revelation, Jesus is called "the Amen" (3:14). This was a divine title, signifying the divine person through whom salvation comes. The title originates in a reference in the book of Isaiah (65:16), where "Amen" is a title of God: the God of Truth. In Isaiah, the reference comes just before God promises to make a new heaven and a new earth, which is seen as fulfilled in the book of Revelation (21:1).

The *Catechism of the Catholic Church* defines Jesus Christ as "the definitive 'Amen' of the Father's love for us." It adds that Jesus takes up and completes our own "Amens":

> For all the promises of God find their Yes in him. That is why we utter the Amen through him, to the glory of God.
>
> — No. 1065

So when early Christians used the Amen, they weren't just refer-ring to the end of a blessing, linked to God's power and faithfulness. They were adding all those new meanings revealed by Jesus — and their own beliefs about him as the bringer of salvation — into the meaning of the ancient word. The early Christian's Amen at the end of prayers meant several things, including:

- "This is the truth, revealed by Christ."
- "This is truth because God's power, revealed in Jesus Christ, is present here."
- "I believe this, in Christ and through the Spirit."

So, in short, the Hebrew Amen became a Christian's true profession of faith, a creed in itself.

Now the Amen didn't enter the creeds — the formal professions of faith — right away. For example, in the *Didache*, the Amen appears only once, in conjunction with a prayer for the Lord to come soon: the *maranatha*. (The *Didache* also includes a rendition of the Lord's Prayer, without using the Amen.)

However, it didn't take long for the Amen to become part of professions of faith. One of the most famous professions from the early Church comes to us from the record of the martyrdom of St. Polycarp (bishop of Smyrna and one of the great Apostolic Fathers) in A.D. 155. At eighty-eight years of age, he was sentenced to be burned at the stake. His captors allowed him to make a final prayer before they lit the pyre. (He did not die in the fire, but had to be stabbed to death.) Polycarp's words, thanking God for allowing him to die in this sacrificial fashion, have been recorded:

> O Lord God Almighty, the Father of Thy beloved and blessed Son Jesus Christ, through whom we have received the knowledge of Thee . . . I bless Thee that Thou hast granted me this day and hour, that I might receive a portion amongst the number of martyrs in the cup of Christ unto resurrection of eternal life, both of soul and of body, in the incorruptibility of the Holy Spirit. . . . For this cause, yea and for all things, I praise Thee, I bless Thee, I glorify Thee, through the eternal and heavenly High-priest, Jesus Christ, Thy beloved Son, through whom with Him and the Holy Spirit be glory both now [and ever] and for the ages to come. Amen.[17]

The Amen gradually entered private Christian prayer and public worship over the centuries. Today, it is used for blessings, at the conclusion of sacraments, at the Consecration at Mass, at the reception of Communion, and at the conclusions of all our prayers. All its many layers of meaning come into play in each of these places.

Each time we say "Amen," it is done as the *Catechism of the Catholic Church* says about all creeds:

Thus the Creed's final "Amen" repeats and confirms its first words: "I believe." To believe is to say "Amen" to God's words, promises and commandments; to entrust oneself completely to him who is the Amen of infinite love and perfect faithfulness.

— No. 1064

Most of us may not remember — or have the time — to say a creed every day, but most of us can manage to say some sort of prayer each day. And as we end it with the Amen, we might be able to take a moment to remember to look at our beliefs, voiced in that prayer, and truthfully add, "Sincerely (all) yours."

CHAPTER 14

Whodunit — The Mysteries
of the Rosary

We now turn our attention to the actual mysteries of the Rosary — twenty in all. As Sherlock Holmes would say, "The game's afoot." So let's explore:

The Joyful Mysteries, revealing the wonder of the Incarnation and the childhood of Jesus.

- The Annunciation (Luke 1:26–38)
- The Visitation (Luke 1:39–56)
- The Nativity (Luke 2:1–20)
- The Presentation (Luke 2:22–38)
- The Finding of Jesus in Temple (Luke 2:41–52)

The Luminous Mysteries, showing Jesus's ministry, where the Good News was first proclaimed and God's healing love revealed.

- Jesus's Baptism (Mark 1:9–11; Matthew 3:13–17; Luke 3:21–22)
- The Wedding at Cana (John 2:1–11)
- The Proclamation of the Kingdom, encompassing the events of Jesus's teaching and healing ministry as recorded in the four Gospels
- The Transfiguration (Mark 9:2–8; Matthew 17:1–8; Luke 9:28–36)
- The Institution of the Eucharist (Mark 14:22–25; Matthew 26: 26–29; Luke 22:15–20; 1 Corinthians 11:23–26)

The Sorrowful Mysteries, which take us to witness Jesus's suffering and death, the first half of the great Paschal Mystery that fully restored humanity's relationship with God.

- The Agony in the Garden (Matthew 26:36–46; Mark 14:32–42; Luke 22:39–46)
- The Scourging (Matthew 27:26; Mark 15:15; John 19:1)
- The Crowning with Thorns (Matthew 27:27–31; Mark 15:15–20; John 19:2–5)
- Christ Carries the Cross (Matthew 27:32; Mark 15:21; Luke 23:26–32; John 19:17)
- The Crucifixion (Matthew 27:33–56; Mark 15:21–41; Luke 23:33–49; John 19:18–30)

The Glorious Mysteries complete the second half of the Paschal Mystery that restored us to union with God. These show the institution of the Church and how a share in the power and glory of God, revealed in the Risen Christ, is offered to all, starting with his Blessed Mother.

- The Resurrection (Matthew 28:1–10; Mark 16:1–11; Luke 24:1–12; John 20:1–18)
- The Ascension (Mark 16:19–20; Luke 24:50–53: Acts 1:1–12)
- Pentecost (John 20:22; Acts 2:1–13)
- The Assumption of the Blessed Virgin. While not recorded in Scripture, this mystery is a long-standing tradition of the Church, formally proclaimed as an infallible teaching by Pope Pius XII, in *Munificentissimus Deus* on November 1, 1950.
- The Coronation of Mary. Again not in the canon of Scripture, this is also as a long-standing belief of the Church that dates back to at least the sixth century. This mystery was reinforced by the Second Vatican Council, which called Mary "Queen over all things" (*Lumen Gentium*, No. 59). In that same document, the Fathers of the Council said that Mary's glory in heaven "is the image and beginning of the Church as it is to be perfected in the world to come" (No. 68).

A good mystery intrigues us, because we can see ourselves in the action. In each mystery of the Rosary, divine love and the plan of salvation are revealed in the events of human life — in events that draw us in because they are similar to our own experiences, but highlighted by the presence of God. We can all relate to a birth, a wedding, a meal, even the sorrows of suffering and death. And we long to see the answers that God is ready to reveal within these events.

The word "mystery" comes to us primarily from the Greek word *musterion*, which is the earliest version of the word. But since *musterion* (or *mysterion*, as it appears in some early writings) refers to something that has been kept secret — it was used especially in reference to pagan rites that one needed to be initiated into — it may not seem to be quite the right word for our exploration of the Rosary.

However, some early Christian writers *did* use the word *mysterion* to refer to the revealed, sometimes sublime, truths of the Gospel. And this is fitting for the mysteries of the Rosary, since those who pray the Rosary are certainly waiting upon the Lord and seeking to learn from him through his teachings recounted in the Gospels.

Like any good mystery story, the mysteries of the Rosary need reflection. We need to sit and ponder them, studying them under the spyglass of faith, just as a detective looks at clues that, in turn, reveal "whodunit."

All good mystery stories have a Who, What, Why, Where, and How. Each of the mysteries of the Rosary do as well.

THE MYSTERIOUS "WHO"

The biggest "who" in all of them in the Rosary is Christ; all the other "whos" that appear in the Rosary's mysteries point to him. We have the angel Gabriel naming Jesus as Savior, Elizabeth calling him "my Lord," and the aged Simeon proclaiming Jesus as "a light for revelation to the Gentiles, and for glory to thy people Israel" (Luke 2:32). Seeing this Light revealed — meeting Christ the Lord, both in the Gospels and in our own lives — reveals the divine "whodunit" we are supposed to meet as we meditate on each Rosary mystery.

From the joy of birth and new life, to weddings and meals, through suffering and death, Jesus in the Gospels revealed the light of God's presence at work in the world in a new way. Therefore everything about the Rosary, as it focuses us on studying the events of the Gospels, speaks to us of Christ. Some people might think that Mary is the Who of the Rosary, since this is the greatest of the Marian prayers. But Mary's role is more that of the great detectives — she is the spyglass that "magnifies" the Lord. This is why she is our guide in the meditations of the Rosary.

WHAT

There are quite a few "whats" (and "whens") going on in the Rosary. Some of them are actual happenings and events — so we have the "what" of the Annunciation, the ministry of Christ, the events of his death and resurrection, and the coming of the Spirit. But these are just facets of the main "what" of the Rosary: God's plan for salvation as it was revealed by Christ. As Pope Paul VI noted in his own reflection on the Rosary, "The orderly and gradual unfolding of the Rosary reflects the very way in which the Word of God, mercifully entering into human affairs, brought about the Redemption."[18]

HOW

In any good mystery, the detective has to show us how "the deed was done." In the same way, Mary reflects upon what her Son revealed of God's plan, the events of the salvation story by which God redeems creation. Jesus, through his life on earth, showed us "the Way" that leads through normal human existence onward to what God had always planned for us: life and eternal glory with God in a union of divine love. In fact, early Christians were sometimes called followers of the Way (Acts 9:2 and 24:22), and were distinguished by the "how" of their way of life: "devoted to the apostles' teaching and fellowship, to the breaking of bread and the prayers" (Acts 2:42).

Jesus, himself a carpenter who knew the "how" of making things, gave his followers the blueprints that showed them How to live the plans of the eternal Kingdom. Mary knew this when she told us in John's Gospel to follow those blueprints: "Do whatever he tells you" (John 2:5).

WHERE

Those first followers of Christ were found in Jerusalem. However, there are several "wheres" in the mysteries of the Rosary. There are the locations of events: Bethlehem, Nazareth, Jerusalem, Calvary, the Galilean countryside. But again, there is a bigger, broader Where — and our great sleuth, Mary, shows us that place, too: "And Mary kept all these things, *reflecting on them in her heart*" (Luke 2:19, emphasis added).

It's no mystery that we now call Mary the Immaculate Heart, and honor Jesus's Sacred Heart in a feast one day before that of her Immaculate Heart. In praying the mysteries of the Rosary, we have drawn closer to the hearts of Jesus and Mary and find there a deeper understanding of the Gospels, which reveal the plan of salvation. Reflecting on the Gospels in our hearts is the "where" of all true prayer.

WHY

The Gospels reveal "the Way, the Truth, and the Life." And that is the Why behind praying the mysteries of the Rosary over again and again: we are reflecting on the mysteries of the Gospels. We want those teachings of the life of Christ to change our hearts — and our very lives. As St. Thérèse of Lisieux said of the Gospel message: "(It's) the Gospels that occupy my mind when I'm at prayer . . . I'm always finding fresh lights there; hidden meanings which had meant nothing to me before."[19]

It may be elementary, but it remains far better for our souls than any best-seller whodunit.

CHAPTER 15

Mirror, Mirror, in My Hand —
The Joyful Mysteries

In her *Magnificat* (Luke 1:46:55), Mary said she magnified the Lord. Like a magnifying lens, all her focus was directed upon the Lord and his will for her. The same can be said about the Rosary. It's a Marian prayer, but it's not about Mary. It's about Christ — and it brings the life of Christ into focus. The whole purpose of praying the mysteries of the Rosary is to reflect upon the life of Christ and the promise of the Gospel. We look at Christ's life, through Mary's, so that we may become like Mary, who "kept all these things, reflecting on them in her heart" (Luke 2:19).

Pope Pius XII, in 1946, called the Rosary a "compendium of the entire Gospel."[20]

The Rosary gives us a way of contemplating the entire Gospel in just four sets of mysteries. And, as we discover when using any good magnifying lens, we find that each set of mysteries offers its own particular point of focus.

The Joyful Mysteries present the wonder of the Incarnation and the childhood of Jesus, who "advanced in wisdom ... before God and man" (Luke 2:52). These mysteries are the Annunciation, the Visitation, the Nativity, the Presentation, and Finding Jesus in the Temple. The five decades of the Joyful Mysteries look at a very special part of the Gospels, the infancy narratives, which appear in only two of the four Gospels. They cover the first twelve years of Our Lord's life, and Mary plays a large role in these narratives.

The Joyful Mysteries and their corresponding Gospel readings are:

- **The Annunciation**, Luke 1:26–38; Matthew 1:18–24
- **The Visitation**, Luke 1:39–56
- **The Nativity**, Luke 2:1–20; Matthew 1:25, 2:1–12
- **The Presentation**, Luke 2:22–38
- **The Finding of Jesus in Temple**, Luke 2:41–52

The Gospel of Luke is the major source of reference for these five mysteries. Only Matthew and Luke relate events of Jesus's early life. And only Luke presents the events as Mary would have experienced them.

The infancy narratives are a special part of the Gospels. In their own way, they present the entire Gospel message, since they recount the beginning of our salvation, hint at the ministry and sufferings of the Lord Jesus, and reveal glints of the glory of salvation that will be offered to all people.

The Joyful Mysteries, like the infancy narratives, serve three main purposes. They:

- present a bridge between the Old and New Testaments;
- present the major themes of the entire Gospel;
- foreshadow the cross and Resurrection.

In the Joyful Mysteries and the infancy narratives we see the fulfillment of the promises of the Old Testament:

There is the acknowledgment of Jesus as Lord by the last of the Old Testament prophets — John the Baptist, while still in his mother's womb.

Mary's *Magnificat* echoes the Old Testament words of Hannah (1 Sam 2:1–10), the mother of Samuel. Samuel was the last of the Judges of Israel and the first of its major prophets. It was Samuel who anointed David, the ancestor of Jesus, as King of Israel.

The angels of the infancy narratives recall the angelic messengers in the Old Testament — the angels of Jacob's vision of a heavenly ladder; the angel (Raphael) who journeyed with Tobit and protected his marriage to Sarah; the angel who stayed Abraham's hand as he was about to offer up his only son, Isaac; and even the angels who barred Adam and Even from Eden. The angel Gabriel — whose name means "God is my strength" — who appears to Mary, also had a role in the Old Testament visions of Daniel revealing the "End of Days" when one "like a son of man" will appear (Daniel 7:13).

Each of the four Gospels has a certain way of presenting Jesus. For Luke's Gospel, which is the primary source for our knowledge of Jesus's birth and childhood, this can be seen in its themes of fulfillment, mercy, joy, and the journey toward salvation. From Gabriel's first words to Mary at the Annunciation to the dying Christ's good news to the repentant thief, and all the healings and parables in between, we can see these themes. So it is not unusual that we see these same themes reflected in the Joyful Mysteries of the Rosary.

The First Joyful Mystery, the Annunciation, has an angel telling Mary not to be afraid because she has found favor with God and is soon to be filled with the Holy Spirit. This foreshadows the angels at the tomb reassuring the fearful women that the powerful promise of God has indeed been fulfilled and Jesus has risen (Luke 24:4–9).

The Second Joyful Mystery, the Visitation, shows us Mary hastening to Elizabeth, an elderly woman in need, foreshadowing Jesus's healing outreach to the poor. And the joy of the two women sharing the good news of God's mercy foreshadows the joy of all those whose lives were changed by the presence of Jesus (Luke 1:39–56).

The Third Joyful Mystery, the Nativity announcement, first revealed to poor shepherds, continues throughout the Gospels as the Good News was announced by Jesus first and most often to the poor, the captives, the blind, and the oppressed (cf. Luke 4:18–19).

The Fourth Joyful Mystery, the Presentation of the Child at the Temple, reveals the universal mission of Christ "a light for revelation to the Gentiles, and for glory to thy people Israel" (Luke 2:32).

The Fifth Joyful Mystery, the Finding in the Temple, foreshadows both the loss and sorrow of Calvary and the joyful healings of

Jesus's ministry and the final glory of the reunions at Easter (Luke 2:41–52).

Not only do the Joyful Mysteries offer a bridge between Old Testament promises and New Testament fulfillment; they also offer a bridge to the other mysteries of the Rosary, especially the Luminous Mysteries, with their focus on the ministry of Christ, and the Sorrowful Mysteries, with their focus on the cross. It takes but a few moments to see these other mysteries only half-hidden in the familiar Christmas images of the infancy narratives and their corresponding Joyful Mysteries:

- **Angels**: Angels appear at key moments throughout Jesus's life: to announce his birth to Mary (the first Joyful Mystery), Joseph, and the shepherds (the third Joyful Mystery); near the start of Jesus's mission (the first Luminous Mystery) after his forty days in the wilderness where "angels ministered to him" (Mark 1:13); and in the garden (the first Sorrowful Mystery) as he began his agony and was in need of strength and comfort (Luke 22:43).

- **Star and Magi**: Only Matthew mentions a star or wise men bearing gifts (part of the third Joyful Mystery). These serve two purposes. The sighting of the Star by those who are not Jews indicates that Gentiles will recognize God's power and receive the Gospel message. (See the story of the pagan prophet Balaam foreseeing a star in Num 24:17). Likewise, Matthew's wise men are Gentiles from the East, most likely astrologers from Persia. For Matthew, they represent all those who will receive the Gospel. In calling Jesus "the newborn King of the Jews" and presenting him with the royal burial gift of myrrh, the Magi also allude to the Cross, which bore the same inscription — "The King of the Jews" (the fifth Sorrowful Mystery).

- **Mary**: Not only does Mary appear as Christ's Mother but she also serves, especially in Luke's Gospel, as the ideal image of discipleship for all followers of Christ. From the Annunciation and her *fiat* (agreement), to the Visitation and her *Magnificat*, to her acceptance of Simeon's words and her diligent search for her twelve-year-old son while he was "about his Father's business" (Luke 2:49), to her key role at the wedding at Cana and through to her faithful position at the Cross, Mary presents a model for all who will follow her son.

Pope Paul VI reminded us of Mary's role as a disciple when he wrote that Mary, in living her own life, was an example of faithful discipleship:

> [S]he fully and responsibly accepted the will of God (cf. Luke 1:38), because she heard the word of God and acted on it, and because charity and a spirit of service were the driving force of her actions. She is worthy of imitation because she was the first and the most perfect of Christ's disciples.[21]

- **Herod**: Herod the Great serves more than a historical purpose in Matthew's infancy narrative. In seeking to destroy the Messiah by murdering the male babies of Bethlehem, Matthew's Herod reminds us of the Egyptian pharaoh who sought to destroy the hope of the people of Israel by killing Hebrew infants. Yet God saved Moses from that king. For Matthew, Jesus is the new Moses, the one who will bring his people to the eternal Promised Land of God's kingdom. Herod — the builder of the great Temple where Jesus is brought as a child (the fourth and fifth Joyful Mysteries) also foreshadows the Herod of the Passion narratives, Herod Antipas, a son of Herod the Great. Finally, the soldiers murdering those innocent children of Bethlehem remind us that Jesus has only escaped the hands of soldiers for a time (the second Sorrowful Mystery).
- **The Temple**: For Jews, the Temple in Jerusalem was God's dwelling place on earth, and Luke uses that as a message in his infancy narrative. In the Temple, the Holy of Holies resides. In the infancy narratives, God's eternal presence dwelling among his people is seen fully in Jesus. This is why

Luke tells us of Jesus coming to the Temple in the first days of his Incarnation (the fourth Joyful Mystery). The Temple remained central throughout Jesus's life and ministry, from his visit there at the age of twelve (the fifth Joyful Mystery) to the cleansing of the Temple, the story of the widow's mite, and his teaching in Solomon's Portico (the third Luminous Mystery). After his Resurrection and Ascension, it is near the Temple that the disciples gather as they await the Holy Spirit, and, after Pentecost (the first three Glorious Mysteries), they are found teaching in the Temple area.

Using only these few examples, we can see that, even if we chose only to reflect on the Joyful Mysteries, we would still find ourselves on a bridge that leads us to the entire story of Christ's mission — from the announcing of the Good News and Emmanuel (God with us) to the spread of the Gospel to the entire world. Reflecting on just these five mysteries can bring us so much closer to understanding Jesus's entire earthly life.

Who would have thought so much insight could be reflected by just fifty small beads held in your hand?

CHAPTER 16

Our Work Orders — *The Luminous Mysteries*

On October 16, 2002, in the twenty-fifth year of his pontificate, Pope John Paul II issued his apostolic letter on the Rosary, *Rosarium Virginis Mariae*, to announce the Holy Year of the Rosary (October 2002–October 2003). In that letter, he proposed a change to the 500-plus-year tradition of the Rosary: the addition of the Luminous Mysteries, or as he called them, "the Mysteries of Light."

The late pope said that the addition of these mysteries was not meant to say anything against the traditional fifteen mysteries of the Rosary, but "to give it fresh life and to enkindle renewed interest in the Rosary's place within Christian spirituality as a true doorway to the depths of the Heart of Christ, ocean of joy and of light, of suffering and of glory."[22]

In this, Pope John Paul drew upon the work of Blessed George Preca, founder of the Society of Christian Doctrine, who had proposed "the mysteries of light" in 1957. Since its roots in the thirteenth to fifteenth centuries, the Rosary had been formatted around 150 prayers — following the tradition of 150 psalms. As such, they had always contemplated the Gospel and the life of Christ through the eyes of Mary. However, since Mary was not present — at least in the Gospel recordings — at most of the public ministry of Christ, Pope John Paul felt that contemplation upon these aspects of Jesus life needed more emphasis.

"Certainly the whole mystery of Christ is a mystery of light," the pope wrote. "He is the 'light of the world' (John 8:12). Yet this truth emerges in a special way during the years of his public life, when he proclaims the Gospel of the Kingdom."[23]

The pope felt it was important to add to the traditional meditations by focusing on "the mysteries of Christ's public ministry between his Baptism and his Passion," in order to learn more about "the person of Christ as the definitive revelation of God."[24]

Wanting to bring a sharper focus upon Jesus's mission on earth, Pope John Paul proposed using the Rosary to highlight five events in Jesus's public life: the Baptism in the Jordan; the great sign at the wedding of Cana; the proclamation of the Kingdom of God; the Transfiguration; and the Institution of the Eucharist.

Pope John Paul intended, through the Luminous Mysteries, to remind us of how Jesus Christ's saving actions were revealed in history, and are still active and being revealed to us today. The Kingdom of God is present to us in our daily lives as it was to the people living in Jesus's time. Pope Paul VI, in his encyclical on Marian devotions, *Marialis Cultis*, also noted how all the mysteries of the Rosary show us how "the Word of God, mercifully entering into human affairs, brought about the Redemption" (No. 45).

The Luminous Mysteries, showing Jesus's ministry, are:

- **The Baptism of Jesus** (Mark 1:9–11; Matthew 3:13–17; Luke 3:21–22)
- **The Wedding at Cana** (John 2:1–11)
- **The Proclamation of the Kingdom**, encompassing Jesus's teaching and healing ministry (the Gospels of Matthew, Mark, Luke, and John)
- **The Transfiguration** (Mark 9:2–8; Matthew 17:1–8; Luke 9:28–36)
- **The Institution of the Eucharist** (Mark 14:22–25; Matthew 26: 26–29; Luke 22:15–20; 1 Corinthians 11:23–26)

As we contemplate these Luminous Mysteries, we grow in understanding of how Jesus continues this through his direct action in our lives, especially visible to us through the sacraments.

Sacraments are how God shares divine life with us. They bring us grace, healing, and nourishment. They give us the fuel that we need to energize us to follow the mission of Jesus. They, as the *Catechism of the Catholic Church* tells us, "sustain us on the way" (No. 2030).

Reflecting upon the Luminous Mysteries helps us to see more clearly this link between the Gospel and the sacraments, both in Jesus's time and, more importantly, in our lives. The seven sacraments — all instituted by Jesus during his earthly mission — are Baptism, Eucharist, and Confirmation (the sacraments of initiation); Reconciliation and Anointing (the sacraments of healing); and Marriage and Holy Orders (the sacraments of service and mission). We can see each of them playing a role in the various Mysteries of Light.

The First Luminous Mystery, Jesus's Baptism, clearly shows a link to the sacraments of Baptism and Confirmation. Not only does Jesus descend into the waters, thus making them holy for all who will follow him, he also makes those waters a pathway to our own mission of life in Him. The Spirit coming upon Jesus in love, affection, and strength was also given to each of us at Baptism. The *Catechism of the Catholic Church* points out how, by our baptism, we are "sacramentally assimilated to Jesus, who in his own baptism anticipates his death and resurrection. The Christian must enter into this mystery of humble self-abasement and repentance, go down into the water with Jesus in order to rise with him, be reborn of water and the Spirit so as to become the Father's beloved son in the Son and 'walk in newness of life.'" (No. 537).

Our baptismal call is the touchstone to which we return again and again to renew ourselves. Each Sunday, as we enter church, we touch the holy water, reminding ourselves of our baptism and our desire to be cleansed and renewed in Christ. Then, in reciting the Creed at Mass, we renew our baptismal promises and reorient ourselves on the journey of faith.

The Second Luminous Mystery, the Wedding at Cana, reveals Jesus at one of the most joyful events of human life. This wedding, recorded in John's Gospel, took place at the start of Jesus's public life. The *Catechism of the Catholic Church* (No. 1613) reminds us that the Church views this as confirming "the goodness of marriage" and that marriage is an effective sign of the presence of Christ in our world.

In marriage, the members of the couple are the ministers of the sacrament, and it is from their union that new life flows. In this, they share directly in the creative work of the Trinity. Jesus, present at the wedding at Cana and turning water into wine, revealed the divine creative work in the context of the human creative ceremony. We who share in the creative work of God are placed right in the midst of this, reminded that Christ worked with something as everyday as water used for washing.

The wedding feast of Cana also hints at the coming institution of the Sacrament of the Altar in its changing of water into wine. In the future, Jesus will take wine and change it into his own blood in the context of a meal. At each Mass, we remember that Cana meal and, through God's creative work and the work of our own hands, we foretaste the wine of the eternal wedding banquet of the Lamb.

The Third Luminous Mystery, the Proclamation of the Kingdom, encompasses all Jesus's work of teaching and healing. Countless lessons, sayings, and healings make up the mosaic of Jesus's ministry. Pope John Paul, in citing this mystery, called Jesus's ministry on earth "the inauguration of that ministry of mercy which he continues to exercise until the end of the world, particularly through the Sacrament of Reconciliation."[25] The healings of Jesus also reflect the sacrament of Anointing of the Sick, the second sacrament of healing.

When reflecting upon this mystery of the Rosary, we should strive to remember that, during his ministry, Jesus sent out his disciples to preach and to heal. Before his Ascension, he did the same. In the same way, we are sent out on the mission of healing and teaching in order to become Christ to others.

The Fourth Luminous Mystery, the Transfiguration, does not link as readily to any one sacrament as do the previous Mysteries of Light. However, since the Transfiguration fully revealed the glorified Christ, it points us toward the goal of all the sacraments: to reveal the kingdom of God in our world, and to show forth our own glorified destiny of complete union with God. This mystery also indicates the call to ministry, first through the presence of Moses and Elijah — the Deliverer of the Old Testament and the greatest prophet of Hebrew Scriptures — and then as Peter, James, and John are called down from the mountain to continue the journey to the cross.

However, it is not just those called to Holy Orders who are sent to reveal the Light of Christ. This is a call that all the baptized share. The Fathers of Vatican II reminded us:

> [All the People of God] are in their own way made sharers in the priestly, prophetical, and kingly functions of Christ; and they carry out for their own part the mission of the whole Christian people in the Church and in the world.[26]

The vision of the glorified Christ serves to lead us onward in that mission.

The Fifth Luminous Mystery, the Institution of the Eucharist, has the clearest link to the sacraments — the Eucharist, which Vatican II called "the summit toward which the activity of the Church is directed" and "the font from which all her power flows."[27] Each time we eat and drink the Body and Blood of Christ, we approach this font and grow from it, becoming more and more like him.

In the first days of the Church, the Eucharist was part of a larger meal, called the *agape* (or "love") feast. How widespread these feasts were is open to debate, but we know that they did include many foods. And they were intended to allow everyone to join in, with each person contributing what they could to the meal. For the poorer members of the community, the common meal, including the central event of the Eucharist, was truly a moment of being filled and a source of support and love; for the richer members of the community, it was a moment of giving and sharing in the generosity of Christ.

In this sacrament, Jesus contributes his very life so that we might have the strength to spread the Good News to the poor, the sick, the outcast, and all in need of new life. In the same way, we who have received the divine life are called to carry it to others.

In a special way, this is also true for those in Holy Orders. Since the Last Supper of the Lord was also the day on which the priesthood was instituted, this mystery carries a special reflection for those in priestly ministry.

The Mysteries of Light, shining forth in everyday life — at a wedding, at a meal of bread and wine, on a mountaintop, or in the depths of a river like the Jordan — transform that everyday life into something extraordinary. Reflecting upon the mysteries can transform us into people energized to do extraordinary things. Like Moses who was sent to free God's people, we are sent. Like Elijah in the desert, we are told to "Arise and eat, else the journey will be too great for you" (1 Kings 19:7). And like those at the Last Supper, we are filled and sent out to bring God's grace — God's very life — to others on the journey.

CHAPTER 17

The End Is Not the End —
The Sorrowful Mysteries

Until the recent addition of the Luminous Mysteries, the Rosary's sequence for centuries was to follow the recitation of the Joyful Mysteries with the Sorrowful Mysteries. Joy turns to sorrow. As it so often does in human life, the angel songs of Nativity are barely still before the hushed trembling of Good Friday comes upon us.

When we looked at the Joyful Mysteries, we explored the infancy narratives. The infancy narratives foreshadow the Passion narrative. Even though the ministry of Jesus — as shown in each Luminous Mystery of his teaching and healing — falls in between, the shadow of the Cross is always present. It's not quite as simple as Shakespeare said in *Romeo and Juliet*, that "we are born to die" — because, as we see with Jesus, death is not the end of life but the hour of glory that leads to eternity. Still, the presence of the cross is always there, glimpsed throughout the Gospels, from Bethlehem to Jerusalem.

One meditation that helps us to focus upon this is the devotion called the Seven Sorrows of Mary, a feast that the Church celebrates on September 15. This feast, long honored in Europe and by various religious orders — such as the Servites, founded in 1304 — was extended to the entire Church by Pope Pius VII in 1814.

The Seven Sorrows (or Seven Dolors) are a meditation on how Mary's joyful role of motherhood came at a high cost. Reflection on these Sorrows, which often parallel the mysteries of the Rosary, can show how the joy of the beginning is never really lost but, instead, mingles with sorrow throughout the Gospels and continues to hint at the glory to come. Like the water turned to wine in the Second Luminous Mystery, the joys and sorrows of everyday life always hint at what they are destined to become in the Light of Christ's resurrection: glorious.

The most commonly accepted list of **Seven Sorrows** is:

- The Prophecy of Simeon
- The Flight into Egypt
- The Loss of Jesus in the Temple
- Meeting Jesus on the Way to Calvary
- The Crucifixion
- The Taking Down (Descent) from the Cross
- The Burial of Jesus

Of all the events in Mary's life that are paired with her Son, we most often seem to focus on her sorrows. No doubt this is part of the reason why, alongside the Greek Orthodox altar that stands over the rock of Calvary in the Church of the Holy Sepulchre in Jerusalem, we find the Portuguese altar of the Sorrowful Mother (*Stabat Mater*). The statue's heart is pierced by the sword of Simeon's prophecy (Luke 2:35), heard of in the fourth Joyful Mystery, but surrounded by golden hearts topped with crosses, rising around her star-crowned head. The sword, the stars, and the hearts reflect shimmers of candlelight from the silver-gilt of the nearby Greek altarpiece and hint at the glory of the nearby tomb of the risen Christ.

So it is with the Sorrows of Mary. Many sorrows touched Mary's life, but always the actions of God were there, sending glimmers of joy and even glory into the shadows of pain, fear, and suffering. The flight into Egypt comes immediately after the joyful mysteries of the Nativity and the Presentation at the Temple; the loss of the boy Jesus in the same Temple is, three days later, followed by the happy reunion of the fifth Joyful Mystery's Finding in the Temple; and the wonder of water made into wine foreshadows the cup of sorrow in the Agony in the Garden of the first Sorrowful Mystery, as well as the glorious "new wine" of the eternal kingdom.

Looking more closely at just the first three Sorrows of Mary reveals how God's actions bring joy to others even through the shadows of fear, pain, or human weakness:

- In the prophecy of Simeon, it is a frail and elderly man who speaks to Mary under the guidance of the Holy Spirit (Luke 2:25–27), and it is the elderly Anna who carries this good news to everyone who will listen;
- During the fear-filled flight into the strange land of Egypt, Joseph is guided by an angel speaking to him and keeping the little family from all harm (Matthew 2:13);
- The loss of the boy Jesus takes place in the Temple, the dwelling place of God on earth, and Jesus spends his time there conversing with the teachers of the Law of Moses — the custodians of the Covenant. Here, even as a frantic Mary and Joseph search, we see elders learning from the living Word of God himself, the bringer of the new covenant. And it is important to remember that the three days of loss experienced by Mary mirror the three days that Jesus will spend in the tomb. We know that the sorrow of separation will again be driven off by the joy of reunion.

Just such reflection upon each of the five Sorrowful Mysteries of the Rosary asks us to seek the presence of God in the midst of pain and death, both in Mary's and Jesus's lives and in our own. Each Sorrowful Mystery calls us to look at what might seem to our eyes now to be an ending and believe that it is only a bridge upon which the action of God will build something new and, ultimately, joyful and even glorious.

In each mystery of the Rosary, we are called to meet the Lord. God's divine love was revealed by Jesus in the events of his own human life, events that are similar to our own, and yet touched fully by the presence of God. While the Sorrowful Mysteries may be difficult, even painful, to contemplate, they are perhaps the most easily identified with our own life experiences. As we contemplate Jesus's sufferings, we also contemplate all the sorrows and deaths we have known.

The Sorrowful Mysteries are:

- **The Agony in the Garden** (Matthew 26:36–46; Mark 14:32–42; Luke 22:40–46)
- **The Scourging** (Matthew 27:26; Mark 15:15; John 19:1)
- **The Crowning with Thorns** (Matthew 27:27–31; Mark 15:15–20; Luke 19:2–5)
- **Christ Carries the Cross** (Matthew 27:32; Mark 15:21; Luke 23:26–32; John 19:17)
- **The Crucifixion** (Matthew 27:33–56; Mark 15:21–41; Luke 23:33–49; John 19:18–30)

The First Sorrowful Mystery, the Agony in the Garden, shows us Jesus experiencing darkness, loneliness, and fear. He awaits his mortal end, contemplating his own death and tempted to turn away. His friends fall asleep, and one even betrays him. Each of us, to some degree, has experienced such loneliness.

And yet, in the midst of sorrow, fear, and anticipated pain, Jesus says "Yes" to God's plan, just as his mother had done at the Annunciation. He allows God's plan to continue. The cup of sorrow does not pass, but, as Luke tells us, God's love remains and is revealed gloriously: "And there appeared to him an angel from heaven, strengthening him" (22:43).

There is a tradition that says Gabriel was that unnamed angel who appeared in Gethsemane. If this is true, we can see yet another link between the Joyful Mysteries and the Sorrowful, since Gabriel is the Angel of the Annunciation, who promised that God would give Jesus the throne of David and that he would rule without end (Luke 2:32–33). Also, since Gabriel's name in Hebrew means "God is my strength," Gabriel's presence would have offered assurance to Jesus that the joy of God's power would not be lost in the dark shadows of a night garden.

The Second Sorrowful Mystery, the Scourging, is mentioned by all the evangelists but Luke — although he does mention a mockery before Herod and his soldiers (Luke 23:11). Again, we can hear whispered echoes from the infancy narratives, where the father of this King Herod (Antipas), Herod the Great, sought the life of the infant Jesus and sent his soldiers to do the awful deed. At that time, Jesus escaped into Egypt, carried by Joseph and led by angels. Now Jesus stands before this son of Herod and is sent on his awful way in the hands of soldiers, but garbed in the robes of a king (Luke 23:11).

The evangelists make short mention of this suffering of Jesus, though historical documents tell us of the horrors of a Roman scourging and how it weakened prisoners to the point of death. Jesus is beaten, he bleeds, and his face — the face of God's glory revealed in the fourth Luminous Mystery of the Transfiguration — is bruised and disfigured. And yet, the glory remains. As Jesus tells Pilate in John's Gospel, an army of angels waits to come at his slightest command (18:36).

As we reflect on this sorrowful mystery, we can also contemplate the times when sickness, injury, and sorrow have disfigured us or those whom we love. And we should remember that angels wait, just beyond our sight, to offer comfort and strength.

The Third Sorrowful Mystery, the Crowning with Thorns, presents us with a cruel picture of mockery. Who hasn't been laughed at or excluded, made the butt of jokes? From playground memories to the isolation of a sick ward, we have heard the words, "*Ecce homo*" (Here is the man), spoken of us. "Here is the one to laugh at," they have said of us. Or, at the least, they have turned away so they cannot see the pain and fear in our eyes.

> He was despised and rejected by men; a man of sorrows, and acquainted with grief; and as one from whom men hide their faces he was despised, and we esteemed him not.
>
> — Isaiah 53:3

This comes from the last of the prophet Isaiah's Suffering Servant Songs. Like the Suffering Servant, revealed in Jesus, we have all been shamed, scorned, or pitied.

And yet, Isaiah also said that God would give his Servant "his portion among the great" (53:12). Isaiah's last prophecy of the Suffering Servant, in the part of his book called "the Book of Comfort," is immediately followed by the joyful promise of the New Zion: "Fear not, for you will not be ashamed" (Isaiah 54:4). God's promise of old — spoken eight centuries before Jesus's birth — rings true in the bloody courtyard of Pilate's fortress. Even in the midst of his agony, Jesus was robed in royal purple and wore a crown, albeit one woven of thorns. He was not put to shame in the eyes of God, even in that shameful place.

As the Lenten hymn sings, "O Sacred Head, surrounded by crown of piercing thorn... yet angel hosts adore thee and tremble as they gaze." Jesus's dignity as the Son of God was never taken from him — could never be taken from him. And because of that truth about Jesus, we know that God also always sees us as his royal children, robed in his love, despite the crowns of suffering pressed down upon our foreheads.

The Fourth Sorrowful Mystery, Christ Carries the Cross, takes us on the journey to the cross with Jesus. In Luke's Gospel, the route to Calvary is long; in John's, it is short. Long or short, we all face a road to Calvary; like Peter, who also died on a cross, we have all been led where you do not want to go (John 21:18). However, Psalm 23, often prayed as a person nears death, reminds us that we do not enter the dark valley alone. Instead, we go with One who has already been there. The joy of companionship, however shadowed, remains with us. Because of Christ, we do not — we cannot — go to our deaths alone.

Only Luke's Gospel gives much description of Jesus's Way of the Cross. Yet, here again, we find the evangelist's themes of fulfillment, mercy, joy, and the journey to salvation — just as we did in the infancy narratives.

Here are the women who weep for Jesus, not unlike anyone who weeps for someone who is ill or dying. We also see the repentant thief, who silences the mocking thief to express his own regrets, only to receive not harsh judgment but the promise of Paradise, even as he is dying.

Luke, Matthew, and Mark all place a soldier by the cross, one who changes his official stance and recognizes Jesus's innocence and glory in the end. Mark's centurion says it best: "Truly this man was the Son of God!" (15:39). And these words come at the very moment when Jesus breathes his last; at the moment of death, a pagan Roman sees the glory of God revealed.

Again, all the evangelists but John mention Simon of Cyrene, who helps Jesus carry the cross. Simon is a model for those who pray about others' pain and sorrow and who will do any act to ease the suffering of another. As Pope John Paul said of him in his apostolic letter on the Rosary:

How could one contemplate Christ carrying the Cross and Christ Crucified, without feeling the need to act as a "Simon of Cyrene" for our brothers and sisters weighed down by grief or crushed by despair?[28]

The Fifth Sorrowful Mystery, the Crucifixion, closes the final chapter of mortal life for Jesus. It is not the peaceful death for which any of us would pray. Yet it is death that each of us has seen and will one day experience firsthand. Here, too, we see that God remains with us, because he has gone ahead of us.

As Jesus said, "When I am lifted up from the earth, I will draw everyone to myself" (John 12:32). Our lives, and our deaths, have been drawn in and united to his. That is more than joy — it is the glory of God made present within sorrow.

This is why the Church teaches that the Paschal Mystery does not end with Jesus's death, but continues into the Resurrection and Ascension. The cross is the throne upon which God revealed Jesus's glory. And because of Jesus's Paschal Mystery, our own deaths become the door to glory. Life did not end in sorrow and death — just as the mysteries of the Rosary do not.

Bishop Frederick Colli of Thunder Bay, Ontario, said this in an Easter homily in 2008:

The celebration of Easter will not take away the burdens and troubles that touch us in our daily journey of life. The celebration reminds us that, even in the midst of struggles and challenging situations, there is hope... linked to the Lord Jesus, any suffering we endure, brings us victory in the end.[29]

These are truly Sorrowful Mysteries, but they stand in the middle of the traditional list of the mysteries of the Rosary. They are not the end — they are a bridge that carries us through darkness to glory.

As Jesus said, "Unless a grain of wheat falls to the ground and dies, it remains just a grain of wheat; but if it dies, it produces much fruit" (John 12:24). Contemplating the Sorrowful Mysteries, we fall to the ground in grief. But we soon rise up to contemplate the new fruit of eternal life revealed in the Glorious Mysteries.

CHAPTER 18

Our Coming Attractions —
The Glorious Mysteries

In St. Mary of the Seven Dolors Church in my hometown, two rows of stained-glass windows line the nave and depict the dramatic events of the life of Mary as revealed in the mysteries of the Rosary. The left windows show the five Sorrowful Mysteries; the right show the five Glorious. Anywhere you stand in the church, you have the Sorrowful Mysteries on one side of you and the Glorious Mysteries on the other. Almost like reflections of each other.

The pairing is appropriate because, as the *Catechism of the Catholic Church* reminds us, the Paschal Mystery of Christ has two sides: death and resurrection (No. 654). Christ's death won our freedom; his resurrection promises us new and eternal life. As Paul said to the Corinthians, we cannot believe in Christ's resurrection and not believe in our own (1 Corinthians 15:12). The Glorious Mysteries remind us that what seemed like the end — the pain and death contemplated in the Sorrowful Mysteries — was only part of the path that is the way of salvation.

The Glorious Mysteries reflect upon the fullness of that salvation, revealed first in the life of Christ and mirrored in the life of his mother. Mary stood at the foot of the cross in John's Gospel, enduring the fifth Sorrowful Mystery, with her soul reflecting her son's sacrifice. While the Gospels do not show Mary present at the Resurrection or the Ascension (the first and second Glorious Mysteries), tradition tells us that the Risen One appeared to her on Easter. (In the Eastern churches, the tradition is that the risen Jesus appeared to Mary on Holy Saturday.) Later, Mary's continuing role in the Glorious Mysteries is seen by her presence in the Upper Room with the disciples when the Holy Spirit overshadows them — as it had done to her at the Annunciation — and fills them with the fire of faith remembered in the third Glorious Mystery.

Pope Paul VI noted:

> The orderly and gradual unfolding of the Rosary reflects the very way in which the Word of God, mercifully entering into human affairs, brought about the Redemption.[30]

This same orderly unfolding of salvation history, contemplated in the first three Glorious Mysteries, shows us what inevitably lies ahead for each of us who follows Christ. God redeemed us by becoming one with us through Christ, so that we might then be forever one with God. As St. Athanasius of Alexandria said back in the fourth century: "God became man so that we might become God" (*Catechism of the Catholic Church*, No. 460).

The Glorious Mysteries promise that what God did for Jesus, God will also do for us. God wishes to draw us to himself for all eternity. The last two Glorious Mysteries, the mysteries of Mary's Assumption and Coronation, reinforce that certainty. What happened to God's own Son — and then to God's mother — will be done for all who hear God's word and keep it.

The Glorious Mysteries are about exaltation. The late philosopher and author, Msgr. Romano Guardini, reminded us that the Paschal Mystery "can be re-enacted in every individual.... The life of Christ is the theme that is given and carried out in everyone anew."[31]

The Glorious Mysteries are:

- **The Resurrection** (Matthew 28:1–10; Mark 16:1–11; Luke 24:1–12; John 20:1–18)
- **The Ascension** (Mark 16:19-20; Luke 24:50–53: Acts 1:16–12)
- **The Descent of the Holy Spirit** (John 20:22; Acts 2:1–13)
- **The Assumption**. While not found in the Gospel, this doctrine was proclaimed as an infallible teaching by Pope Pius XII in

Munificentissimus Deus, on All Saints' Day, November 1, 1950, capping what was already a tradition in the Church.

- **The Coronation of Mary**. Again not found in the Gospel, this teaching of the Church dates back to at least the sixth century.

Each of the five Glorious Mysteries shows us another facet of the culmination of the plan God has for all creation, including each of us. What God did for Jesus and for Mary, he will do for us. Each mystery presents a blazing sign, a revelation of coming attractions each of us will find in the greatest story ever told: this history of salvation and the story of our own coming glory in Christ.

The First Glorious Mystery, the Resurrection, is central to our faith: Christ rose and his resurrection gave us, each and personally, the promise of eternity. As St. Paul said:

> Do you not know that all of us who have been baptized into Christ Jesus were baptized into his death? We were buried therefore with him by baptism into death, so that as Christ was raised from the dead by the glory of the Father, we too might walk in newness of life.
>
> — Romans 6:3–4

Because of Jesus's death and resurrection, we are assured of eternal life — not just in a manner of speaking, but completely and totally, in our very own bodies. As Dominican friar Fr. Bernhard Blankenhorn said in an Easter homily in 2008:

> The resurrection changes everything. It isn't just about Jesus coming back to life. It changes our entire vision of the human body. . . . Salvation isn't just about the soul. It's also about the body . . . because the body matters and was made for glory.[32]

The Second Glorious Mystery, the Ascension — not the Resurrection — completes the drama of Calvary. The Passion and the cross were the beginning of the Ascension — the left side, if you will, of my St. Mary Church. The Resurrection and Ascension, standing on the right side across the aisle from the cross and the tomb, are the other side of the Paschal Mystery. As the *Catechism of the Catholic Church* says:

> The lifting up of Jesus on the cross signifies and announces his lifting up by his ascension into heaven, and indeed begins it.

> — No. 662

The events are tied — because one happened, the other is inevitable in God's plan.

It is because of this that we are assured that we can follow Jesus. St. Thomas Aquinas said that Christ's ascension is the direct cause of our own future ascensions:

> Christ, by once ascending into heaven, acquired for Himself and for us in perpetuity the right and worthiness of a heavenly dwelling place.[33]

The Third Glorious Mystery, the Descent of the Holy Spirit, illuminates that inseparable link between our bodies here and the physical, risen body of Christ— eternally present with God — bringing God's kingdom into everyday life. The Holy Spirit, who came at Pentecost and comes for each of us at baptism, falls upon those who believe in Christ and shares the life of God with them.

Mary is the one who perfectly mirrored this truth all her life. Mary, who had gathered with the disciples in the Upper Room after the Resurrection, had already been overshadowed by the Spirit (the first mystery of the Rosary). She, who had been filled with the Spirit and become the Mother of God, then fulfilled her role as the Mother of the Church when the Spirit returned to overshadow her Son's followers. This is why we do not hear of her again in the Gospels; her role on earth was fulfilled as her spiritual children fully took the role of discipleship upon themselves.

In 1973, the U.S. bishops issued a pastoral letter on Marian devotions and noted a striking resemblance between the Annunciation (the first Joyful Mystery) and this third Glorious Mystery of Pentecost. Calling Mary the "great mother figure of the Church," the bishops noted that Mary, "surrounded by His disciples, prayed for the coming of that same Spirit, in order that the Church, the Body of her Son, might be born at Pentecost."[34]

The Spirit who had overshadowed Mary and anointed Jesus at his baptism in the Jordan (the first Luminous Mystery) — and who fell upon the disciples — now exists within each of us, dwelling in the temples that our bodies became at our own baptisms.

The Fourth Glorious Mystery, the Assumption of Mary, does not reflect a Gospel event. However, honoring Mary's Assumption dates a long way back in history, to at least the fourth century.[35] Official celebrations of the Assumption date to seventh-century Jerusalem, near the site of today's Dormition Basilica. There, the feast was celebrated on August 15 and was first called the Feast of the Dormition (the "Going to Sleep") of Mary. By the eighth century, the word "Assumption" was used.

The fact of the Assumption (from the Latin *assumere*, to take up) flows naturally from the Resurrection promise — and applies that promise to all humanity. While the Assumption of Mary is, as the *Catechism of the Catholic Church* says, "a singular participation in her Son's resurrection," it is also "an anticipation of the resurrection of other Christians" (No. 996).

The Fifth Glorious Mystery, the Coronation of Mary, reflects the high status Mary has held since the earliest centuries of Christian faith. Clearly, Mary was the leader of prayer at the first Pentecost, when the Holy Spirit descended upon the disciples.

However, the feast of the Queenship of Mary on August 22 is one of the newest of the Marian feasts on the liturgical calendar. It was added in 1954 by Pope Pius XII and originally celebrated on

May 31. As part of the liturgical reform following the Second Vatican Council, the feast of Mary's Queenship was moved to August 22, which is the octave of the Assumption.

Mary's queenship, while unique to her, still reveals what awaits us. As the Fathers of Vatican II wrote in their document on the Church:

> The Mother of Jesus, in the glory which she possesses in body and soul in heaven, is the image and beginning of the Church as it is to be perfected in the world to come. Likewise she shines forth on earth until the day of the Lord shall come, a sign of certain hope and comfort to the pilgrim People of God.
> — *Lumen Gentium*, No. 68

We are pilgrims, following signs. In each mystery of the Rosary, we find signs that help us meet the Lord through the eyes and life of Mary, his mother. In the Rosary meditations, the mystery of divine love is revealed in the midst of human life, in daily events similar to our own but lighted fully by God's presence. By reflecting upon her son's life, Mary united herself to God, and the light of God was revealed to her, and in her. God filled Mary with the Holy Spirit and, in proper time, raised her to heaven.

Similar reflection is meant to do the same for us. As we ponder the Gospel events in our hearts, our own lives will begin to reflect Christ's light. In so doing, we act like neon signs, showing that we are aglow with anticipation over the coming of the greatest attraction we could ever witness: God revealing his light and love to us, and in us, just as he did to Mary. All we need to do is take our place in the line of discipleship that Mary started and say, "May it be done to me according to your word" (Luke 1:38).

CHAPTER 19

Pick a Number, Any Number . . . Any Color, Too

"EIGHT"

In competitive ice skating, the figure "8" was part of the compulsory exercises undertaken by figure skaters in training and competition for decades. (It's called "figure skating" because of these compulsory elements, or figures, which were phased out of competition by the 1990s.)

In the world of mathematics and science, "8" turned on its side is the symbol for infinity: ∞. More correctly, it means "without end."

In rosaries, the figure "8" can be part of a marriage.

The Lasso Rosary is a "figure-eight" Rosary often used in Hispanic cultures for the marriage ceremony. *El lazo* is actually a pair of oversized five-decade rosaries, joined together at the center. Lasso Rosaries share a crucifix and the first beads to the Rosary medallion. Each of the two loops is placed over the heads of the bride and groom to symbolize their prayerful union in God.

While the Lasso Rosaries are most often only used at the wedding ceremonies, some couples use them throughout their married lives to pray the Rosary together.

ONE, THREE, FIVE

El lazo is only one of the many variations in Rosary types that deal with numbers. Traditional rosaries, most often the Dominican style, consist of five decades of ten beads each. However, variations range from one to twenty decades in a single Rosary, or contain a different number of beads that do not equal ten (a decade).

The smallest rosaries can fit on your finger. **Ring rosaries** have only one decade, represented by little bumps or beads around the circumference, with a cross the center of the ring. Counting the beads is as simple as twisting the ring with a push of the thumb. Bracelet rosaries are often similar, with more decorative beads.

A variation of the one-decade Rosary for modern times is the **auto rosary.** Similar to the bracelet rosary, it has a clasp in the center which allows the Rosary to be clipped to the rearview mirror or the steering wheel. (One needs to take care before using these; check that they're not against traffic regulations in your area!)

The Crown of Our Lord consists of three decades of ten beads, plus three other beads. It symbolizes the number of years that our Lord was on earth and is meant to be used to meditate on the events of his life.

The Rosary for the Dead has four decades. Its forty beads commemorate the forty hours which Jesus spent in the tomb, when he traditionally traveled in the realm of the dead.

Smaller rosaries such as these are sometime known as chaplets. Technically, any Rosary is a chaplet — which comes from the French word *chapelet*, meaning "wreath." However, chaplets are often based around a specific image of Christ, Mary, or an event in their lives. Thus, there are the Chaplets of Divine Mercy, of the Holy Face, and of the Precious Blood. The Chaplet of the Five Wounds of Christ has five sets of five beads. For Mary, chaplets include the Chaplet of the Immaculate Conception and the Chaplet of the Seven Sorrows.

There are also popular chaplets dealing with saints and angels, such as the Chaplets of Michael, Raphael, and the Holy Angels, and Chaplets of Joseph, Patrick, Philomena, and the Little Flower. There is even a Chaplet of the Holy Ghost.

SIX AND SEVEN

There are six- and seven-decade rosaries that could be thought of as being even more Marian than the very Marian Rosary itself, because these are based on Mary's own life experiences. These include one famous Rosary named for a saint, but based on Mary's life.

The Chaplet (or Crown) of St. Bridget, also called the Brigittine Rosary, is a six-decade Rosary. It contains sixty-three *Ave* beads in total, which honors the tradition that Mary lived for sixty-three years before her Assumption. The six decades are separated by a total of seven Our Father beads, and these are most often used to commemorate the Seven Joys and Seven Sorrows of the Blessed Mother.

Two Rosaries specifically address Mary's sorrows and joys, and each consists of seven sets of prayer beads.

The Servite Rosary is named for the Servants of Mary, whose religious order was officially founded in 1304. Their devotion to Mary and the sorrows she suffered during Christ's Passion are embedded in the Servite Rosary — also called the Seven Sorrows Rosary. This Rosary consists of seven sets of seven beads each.

As noted in Chapter 17, the **Seven Sorrows of Mary** are:

- The Prophecy of Simeon
- The Flight into Egypt
- The Loss of Jesus in the Temple
- Meeting Jesus on the Way to Calvary
- The Crucifixion
- The Taking Down (Descent) from the Cross
- The Burial of Jesus

The Seven Joys of Mary. The Franciscan Order, while devoted to the fifteen-decade Rosary, is also the inspiration behind the seven-decade Rosary called the *Franciscan Crown.* This is also known as the *Seraphic Rosary,* or the Rosary of the Seven Joys of Our Lady, and dates to sometime in the fifteenth century, most often to 1422.

This 1422 date relates to the story behind the seven-decade Rosary: the devotion of a young Franciscan novice. This unnamed man, before entering the Franciscan order, was in the habit of weaving wreaths of roses for a statue of the Virgin Mary. After entering the order, the young man was no longer able to make his flower wreaths, and it greatly disturbed him — to the point that he considered leaving the Franciscans.

However, he then experienced a vision of Mary that told him he would now be weaving her prayer wreaths. Later, as the young man was praying the Rosary, his novice director saw an angel standing near him and weaving a crown of roses, interspersed with golden lilies.

The **Seven Joys of Mary** are:

- The Annunciation
- The Visitation
- The Nativity
- The Adoration of the Magi
- The Finding of the Child Jesus in the Temple
- The Resurrection
- The Assumption and Coronation of the Blessed Virgin

COLORS

While most Rosaries do not have specific colors linked to them, there are a few exceptions. For example, the Chaplet of St. Joseph consists of blue and white beads, to symbolize the purity of Mary's spouse. The Chaplets of the Sacred Heart, Precious Blood, and Five Wounds all have red beads.

Perhaps the most unique color code for a Rosary is that developed by the late Archbishop Fulton Sheen, whose cause for canonization was opened in 2002. While he was serving as the national director of the Society for the Propagation of the Faith, then-Bishop Sheen developed the **Missionary Rosary**. It has five decades, each one of a different color, to represent the five continents. In saying this Rosary, the normal pattern is used.

The colors and continents of the **Missionary Rosary** are:

- Yellow for Asia, where the light of the morning sun begins
- Blue for the islands of the Pacific, or Oceania
- White for Europe, where the Holy Father (who wears white) resides
- Red for North and South America, in honor of the flame of faith brought there by the missionaries
- Green for Africa and its vast grasslands or savannas

From one to twenty, all the colors of the rainbow, symbols of the love between man and woman or the infinity of eternity, each of the many types of rosaries — like the "figure eight" — uses our prayers and meditations to draw us into the love of God which is already wrapped around us. Forever and ever, without end, Amen.

CHAPTER 20

"The Cherry on Top"

My grandmother went to work as a young woman in the midst of the Great Depression, working long hours in downtown Chicago at a major department store. To keep her job, she was required to work her full shift, punch off the time clock, and then work a few more hours — for free.

It might not have been fair, but it kept her job when many others lost theirs or couldn't find work. It brought home the necessities and kept her going day by day. Any overtime pay or bonus she received was never planned on, but it was hoped for. And when it came, it was reason to celebrate. She called it "the cherry on top."

For my grandmother, when all the basics were covered, anything extra was "the cherry on top." It went for fun things, maybe a night of dancing or a new dress. They weren't necessary, but they sure were nice and made each day something to look forward to in tough times.

The Rosary, as a devotional tool, is complete after the Our Fathers, Hail Marys, and Glory Bes are finished. There's nothing more that needs to be added. However, over the years, other prayers have worked their way into the sequence, usually at the end of the traditional meditations. They aren't necessary, but they add the cherry on top of what, for many, is a daily devotion.

The most common prayers added to the end of the Rosary are:

- The Fatima prayers (of which there are seven)
- The Prayer to St. Joseph
- The *Memorare*
- The Prayer to St. Michael

The **Fatima prayers** include five prayers taught to the shepherd children during their famous visions of 1916 and 1917. In 1916, Lucia dos Santos and her cousins, Francisco and Jacinta Marto, experienced apparitions of an Angel of Peace, who prepared them for their visions of the Blessed Mother the following year. This angel taught the children the first two of the Fatima prayers — the Pardon Prayer and the Angel's Prayer. The Decade Prayer, the Eucharistic Prayer, and the Sacrifice Prayer were all taught to the children by the Blessed Mother herself. The final two prayers, the Conversion and Salvation Prayers, were taught to Sister Lucia after she had entered the convent and her two cousins had died.

(On May 13, 2000, Francisco and Jacinta were declared "blessed." Sister Lucia died on February, 13, 2005, and her cause for beatification was opened three years later.)

The Fatima prayers are most often prayed together as a separate chaplet. However, the Decade Prayer is often added to the recitation of the Rosary itself, and prayed after each of the decades. The children of Fatima said that this was according to the request of Mary herself on July 13, 1917. It, as are all Marian prayers, is directed to Jesus.

The Fatima Decade Prayer

O my Jesus, forgive us our sins, save us from the fires of hell, and lead all souls to heaven, especially those in most need of your mercy.

The **Prayer to St. Joseph** is an obvious addition when you consider the Rosary. Given Joseph's role as Mary's spouse and his role in salvation history, to seek his aid while praying with Mary is a natural. There are several prayers of St. Joseph. Pope Leo XIII, in 1889, recommended the following prayer (*Ad te, beate Joseph*) to be used during the month of October, the month of the Rosary:

To you, O Blessed Joseph, we come in our trials, and having asked the help of your most holy spouse, we confidently ask your patronage also. Through that sacred bond of charity which united you to the Immaculate Virgin Mother of God and through the fatherly love with which you embraced the Child Jesus, we humbly beg you to look graciously upon the beloved inheritance which Jesus Christ purchased by his blood, and to aid us in our necessities with your power and strength.

O most provident guardian of the Holy Family, defend the chosen children of Jesus Christ. Most beloved father, dispel the evil of falsehood and sin. Our most mighty protector, graciously assist us from heaven in our struggle with the powers of darkness. And just as you once saved the Child Jesus from mortal danger, so now defend God's Holy Church from the snares of her enemies and from all adversity. Shield each one of us by your constant protection, so that, supported by your example and your help, we may be able to live a virtuous life, to die a holy death, and to obtain eternal happiness in heaven. Amen.

— Prayer as cited at www.dads.org

The Memorare is so named from the first word of the prayer — "remember," or *memorare* in Latin. The prayer is often attributed to St. Bernard of Clairvaux, the great twelfth-century Doctor of the Church. However, this has not been accurately traced; it seems more likely that the association with the name "Bernard" is from the name of the priest who made the prayer popular in the seventeenth century, Fr. Claude Bernard.

Fr. Bernard (d. 1641) was a French priest who devoted his life to serving prisoners, especially those condemned to death. One of his favorite prayers in his ministry was the *Memorare*; in a letter to Queen Anne of Austria, he claimed that reciting the prayer had once saved him from a deathly illness.

The Memorare

Remember, O most gracious Virgin Mary, that never was it known that anyone who fled to your protection, implored your help, or sought your intercession was left unaided.

Inspired by this confidence I fly unto you, O virgin of virgins, my Mother. To you do I come, before you I stand, sinful and sorrowful. O Mother of the Word Incarnate, despise not my petitions, but in your mercy, hear and answer me. Amen.

The Fatima prayers (especially the Decade prayer), the *Memorare*, and the Prayer to St. Joseph all have clear links to Mary. But where is the tie between the Rosary and St. Michael? The reason the **Prayer to St. Michael** is used with the Rosary becomes clearer when you look at how the Prayer to St. Michael is linked to the *Memorare* and to St. Joseph.

Fr. Bernard taught the *Memorare* to prisoners who were about to die. St. Joseph is considered the patron of a happy death, because tradition teaches that he died in the arms of Mary and Jesus. The end of one St. Joseph prayer asks the great foster father of Jesus to embrace Jesus and ask him to return that hug "when I draw my dying breath. St. Joseph, patron of departing souls — pray for me."

The link to St. Michael comes about because of that last moment of life — "the cherry on top" of all our days, if you will. In Catholic tradition, St. Michael is the defender of souls, especially at the moment of death.

While we may most often think of Michael as a warrior angel because of his role as the prince of the angelic defenders of heaven and the story in the book of Revelation (12:7–9), where Michael drives Satan from heaven and casts him into hell, Michael has a lesser-known but long-time role as a patron of the sick.

Near ancient Constantinople, when that city was known as "the Rome of the East," a shrine was located about fifty miles south of the city proper, in Sostenion. Built near a spring of water, the shrine was long dedicated to pagan gods of healing. It was here that the archangel Michael was said to have appeared to the Roman Emperor Constantine (d. 337). The emperor later built a Christian shrine there, called the *Michaelion* in honor of the angel, which became a site of pilgrimage for the sick. Those seeking healing slept inside the church, bathed in the springs, and prayed for a cure. A feast day for the archangel was celebrated there on June 9.

This tradition didn't come out of nowhere or originate with Constantine, however. Even earlier, in the early days of the Church, there was a shrine to St. Michael at Colossae, over the hot springs found there. Legends said that the angel himself had split the rock with lightning when nonbelievers tried to dam those springs and destroy the shrine's church building. The Greek Orthodox Church still keeps the feast of St. Michael on November 8, tracing back to this ancient Greek tradition.

In Egypt, the early Coptic Church placed the River Nile under the protection of St. Michael, because its waters were so vital to the health of the land and people. The feast of St. Michael "at the rising of the Nile" is still observed on November 12.

Later than all of this, in A.D. 590, Western church tradition says the archangel appeared in Rome over the tomb of Hadrian during a procession led by Pope St. Gregory I, undertaken to ask God to end a plague in the city. After the reported angelic appearance, the plague ended, and the mausoleum soon had a new name — *Castel Sant'Angelo* (castle of the Holy Angel) — which it still bears today.

Prayer to St. Michael

St. Michael the Archangel, defend us in battle.
Be our defense against the wickedness and snares of the
     Devil.
May God rebuke him, we humbly pray;
and do thou, O Prince of the heavenly host,
by the power of God, thrust into hell Satan,
and all the evil spirits,
who prowl about the world seeking the ruin of souls. Amen.

Condemned prisoners, the sick, and the dying — all of these pray for mercy as they face the end of life. Whether beseeching the aid of Mary, Joseph, or Michael, we are all really turning to the Lord and asking his mercy. Using these extra prayers of the Rosary, we can present our lives to the Lord, through the intercession of others, and ask that he grant us the ultimate "cherry on top" — everlasting life with him.

CHAPTER 21

Devotions — Stealing Worship from God?

Discussion about prayers to the various saints, including the Blessed Mother, always brings up the question of focus. As Catholics, we've all heard the question from Protestant friends: "Why do you pray to the saints? We only pray to God." Or someone else asks, "Do you worship Mary?"

Even practicing Catholics get confused. In my work as an editor at a Catholic newspaper, I received the following letter from a reader.

> What bothers me the most is the fact that every prayer directed at Mary is a prayer not being directed to GOD the Father. Every minute of a worship service directed at Mary, is a minute of worship taken directly from GOD. Was not the backbone of Jesus's ministry that everything is to be directed to the Father? Did not Jesus direct us to pray to GOD and *only* GOD the Father?
>
> (Emphasis in original)

Part of the difficulty in understanding what Catholics do when we "pray to the saints" comes from understanding what "pray to" means. In our modern understanding of the phrase, we immediately associate it with the word "prayer," which is an act of worship. And worship, for Catholics as well as other Christians, *is* directed only to God.

However, when we are talking about saints, we understand "pray to" as related to the word "pray." The word "pray" comes from Old English, French, Latin, German, and even Sanskrit words meaning "to ask." So, when we pray to Mary or the saints, we are *asking* for their help. (Maybe using the phrase "pray with" instead of "pray to" would make matters easier.)

When you are sick, or have some big problem in your life, don't you ask your friends to pray for you? Why? Doesn't God listen to your own prayers?

Of course, God does. But we ask others to pray for us because we believe that shared prayer is also an act of shared worship and devotion. That is why we gather together for liturgy, as well as for other forms of communal prayer: we believe God calls us into community, to share God's graces with each other. We are the people of God and, as a people, we join together to be with Christ and with each other, offering praise and worship to God, and presenting our needs and concerns.

In fact, Jesus himself *directed* us to pray together: "Where two or three are gathered in my name, there am I in the midst of them" (Matthew 18:20).

So, by joining our prayers together, we join our worship and our needs together. And we don't just do this at the Mass. We also do this through devotions — and the Rosary is one of the most popular of devotions.

We all know what it means to be devoted; there are devoted fans, devoted couples, devoted pets, even golf devotees. They are passionate about the object of their devotions. But the word "devotion" comes from a Latin word meaning, "dedicate by a vow." Eventually, it came to mean devotion, or piety, to God.

The Catholic Encyclopedia defines Catholic devotions as forms of prayer that are not part of the public worship of the Church, such as the Mass or the administration of sacraments. Rather, devotions are spiritual practices that developed as private prayer and later became publicly shared, while still remaining essentially private. As they became publicly shared, these private devotions often developed formalized prayers and styles.

Many such devotions focus on Mary, but many also surround the life of Jesus, such as the Stations of the Cross or Holy Name devotions. And it is here that we find the connection that makes our prayers to Mary and the other saints different from our prayers to God. Mary herself said it best:

"Behold, henceforth all generations will call me blessed; for he who is mighty has done great things for me, and holy is his name."

— Luke 1:48–49

Mary was speaking in the joy of being blessed by God to become the mother of the Lord. She was honoring God, worshiping God, and directing Elizabeth — who had just given her honor by calling her the Mother of the Lord — to do the same, redirect her thoughts to God. Mary was acknowledging the blessings of God and how God had shaped and directed her life.

Mary was greatly honored by God. Through her own prayers and actions throughout her life, that honor was magnified and given back to God. This continues to this day, with any honors directed to Mary — they are ultimately given to God.

The Church even has terms for this: *dulia* and *latria*. Both words come from the Greek and were the subject of much debate by leaders of the early Church, such as St. Augustine, who defined them as obedience (*dulia*) and homage (*latria*). Both words have to do with honor and worship. But *dulia* (which means "service" or "servitude") has to do with the honor one gives to another human being — even though it sometimes meant the honor that a slave gave to a master. Thus, *dulia* is the honor now given to saints. *Latria* always referred to the divine and to the honor given to God alone.

The Church even added another term — *hyperdulia* — which it reserved for Mary, sort of a "super-servitude" to the "Mother of my Lord." It is part of the reason that we call Mary "Our Lady," in the way subjects of earthly kingdoms addressed a queen.

It can get confusing and, with all the prayers, worship, veneration, and honor going around, people who are watching us could easily get confused. However, the Church has always been clear, and the Fathers of the Second Vatican Council only restated it:

> The various forms of piety toward the Mother of God . . . bring it about that, while the Mother is honored, the Son, through whom all things have their being and in whom it has pleased the Father that all fullness should dwell, is rightly known, loved and glorified and that all His commands are observed.
>
> — *Lumen Gentium*, No. 66

In other words, while devotions to Mary and the saints may place us at their disposal — in the way servants or students place themselves under the protection and guidance of lords, ladies, and teachers — those saints, and the great Lady of the Church, properly guide us to God. When we turn to Mary in prayer — especially by praying the Rosary, which reflects on the events of the life of her Son — and ask for her help, Mary does what she has always done. She points to Jesus and tells the devoted servants: "Do whatever he tells you" (John 2:5).

CHAPTER 22

Armed for Battle

Imagine you're on the high seas, off the coast of Greece. A battle is raging about you. You're outnumbered by the superior navy of the Ottoman Turks: they have more than 300 ships, and you don't even have 200. Two of the four divisions of your fleet are late getting into formation, and you are outmaneuvered from the start of the battle. What gets you the victory?

If you're the Holy League, commanded by Don Juan de Austria in the five-hour Battle of Lepanto on October 7, 1571, it's the Rosary.

This major battle was a turning point in the location of world power being centered in the East and moving to West. It kept the Muslims from invading Western Europe and offered the possibility that Christian nations might retake Constantinople. (That attempt failed, but the shift of power to the West continued.)

The major players in the battle were Spain, the Papal States, and the city-states of Venice, Genoa, and Naples. While the battle was raging, Pope Pius V authorized a Rosary procession to take place in St. Peter's Square. (Pope Pius had been a member of the Dominican order, which was dedicated to spreading devotion to the Rosary, so it wasn't surprising that he would turn to this form of prayer in a time of trouble.)

After the battle was won, the pope declared October 7 to be marked as the feast of Our Lady of Victory. Two years later, Pope Gregory XIII changed the name to the Feast of the Holy Rosary. The feast slowly spread through the Western Church and became a universal celebration, under Pope Clement XI, after another victory over the Ottoman Turks in 1716.

For a time, the feast was celebrated on the first Sunday of October, but it was returned to the October 7 date in 1913. In 1969, Pope Paul VI changed the day's name to "Our Lady of the Holy Rosary."

With the feast of the Holy Rosary falling in the month of October, it is not unusual that the entire month of October should become dedicated to the Rosary. This happened in 1883, under Pope Leo XIII.

Known as the Rosary Pope, Leo XIII issued no less than twelve encyclicals on the Rosary, starting in 1883 and following with one nearly each year until 1898. In the first of these encyclicals — *Supremi Apostolatus Officio* — the pope referred to the Rosary as "a most powerful, warlike weapon" to put enemies to flight (4).

More than 100 years later, while not using any martial themes, Pope John Paul did refer to the war of terror that had erupted the year before. In *Rosarium Virginis Mariae*, he placed the Rosary in the midst of countering terrorism:

> The Rosary has many times been proposed by my predecessors and myself as a prayer for peace. At the start of a millennium, which began with the terrifying attacks of 11 September 2001, a millennium which witnesses every day in numerous parts of the world fresh scenes of bloodshed and violence, to rediscover the Rosary means to immerse oneself in contemplation of the mystery of Christ who "is our peace", since he made "the two of us one, and broke down the dividing wall of hostility" (Eph 2:14).
>
> — No. 6

During the World Wars, soldiers often carried rosaries, many made of brass. The center medal of these rosaries was engraved with the time-honored request: "I am a Catholic. Call a priest."

During the Iraq War (officially launched on the feast of St. Joseph in 2003 and formally ended on Aug. 31, 2010), many of the Catholic news wires carried articles about grassroots efforts to send rosaries to troops in a nation where Christian symbols were unwelcome, if not illegal. Many of these rosaries were handmade from twine or string, with knots for beads, since the rattling of wood or plastic or the glint of light on metal might give away troop positions.

When a Rosary is carried into battle — or offered up for troops by those left behind — a glimmer of peace moves over the battle-field because Our Lady of Victory is also the Queen of Peace, and the mother of the Prince of Peace.

CHAPTER 23

Making Scents of Heaven

Did you ever make daisy chains as a child? Or maybe, as I did, you made dandelion chains? They were sure signs of spring, which was like a hint of heaven in the harsh upper Midwest where I grew up.

We started these reflections on the Rosary by noting that "rosary" originally referred to a garland of flowers, only later being transformed into a garland of prayer flowers. So it seems appropriate to end our reflection on the Rosary with flowers.

One of the Virgin Mary's titles is the Mystical Rose.

A rose blooming amidst the thorns is perhaps the best-known floral symbol of the Mother of God, and an analogy to her life. A legend, probably dating to the Middle Ages, says that St. Thomas — never shaking the title of Doubter — did not believe Mary had been raised to heaven and so had her tomb reopened to prove it. What he found inside were roses and lilies.

The link between Mary and roses continued through the centuries. The fourteenth-century poet Dante referred to Mary in his classic *Paradiso* as "the Rose in which the divine Word became flesh."

But the floral association with Mary isn't limited to roses and lilies. So many other flowers have been associated with Mary — both for her personal attributes and her life story — that medieval gardens began to be planted in her memory. First called "St. Mary Gardens," they can be traced to fifteenth-century Scotland and England, where they had been derived from monastery cloister gardens. St. Mary Gardens contain only flowers and plants that are named for Mary or have a Marian legend connected with them.

Today, Mary Gardens are common in many parish landscapes — starting from the first recorded Mary Garden in this country, planted at St. Joseph Church in Woods Hole, Massachusetts, in 1932, through the many gardens inspired by John S. Stokes, Jr., starting with his 1951 Mary's Garden in Philadelphia, Pennsylvania. For the millennium celebration in 2000, a Mary Garden was dedicated at the National Shrine of the Immaculate Conception in Washington, D.C. It was filled with only white and blue flowers, with the white symbolizing the Virgin's purity and blue her royalty, since the color was associated with Byzantine empresses.

So many plants and flowers are associated with Mary that many Mary Gardens — like the one at the National Shrine — can be kept using only a one- or two-color scheme. A garden full of white lilies, white chrysanthemums (a symbol of the Three Kings), white impatiens (symbolizing a mother's love, since they bloom all season), and white roses is just one single-color possibility.

Besides white, purple is also associated with Mary, since purple is the color of sorrow. And the best-known purple flower of Mary is the iris — the royal French *fleur-de-lis*. In the thirteenth-century cathedral of Chartres, France, the rose window depicts Mary holding the Holy Infant surrounded by twelve *fleurs-de-lis*. The purple iris, with its three main purple petals (for the Trinity) and spear-shaped, stiff leaves (representing both royalty and sorrow), give the iris another name: the "sword flower." The name relates to Simeon's prophecy: "And you yourself a sword will pierce" (Luke 2:35).

Also from France comes the Marian name for the blue-purple foxglove, the *Gant de Notre Dame* ("the glove of Our Lady"). Medieval England contributed another name for the violet — "Mary's modesty" — for its low-growing style, shaded by its heart-shaped leaves. The blue delphinium is often called "Mary's tears." Another tradition indicates that Mary used blue lavender, with its strong scent, to wash the baby Jesus's clothes.

Bright colors are also associated with Mary gardens. Pink thrift blossoms are called "Mary's pincushion," and the orange turban lily is called "Our Lady's Tears." Even Shakespeare knew about Mary and the yellow marigolds, which he mentioned in *A Winter's Tale*.

More than flowers are associated with the Blessed Mother. There is also the strawberry, called the "fruitful Virgin" because it bears both white flowers and red fruit at the same time. And a Sicilian legend says that the juniper tree — with its soft interior and sharp needles — opened up to shelter the Holy Family from pursuing soldiers during the Flight to Egypt.

Since the legends about Mary and flowers often include Christ and actually take their meaning from his life and Paschal Mystery, a recent development in Mary Gardens is not surprising: the Rosary Garden.

At St. Francis Xavier Cathedral in Green Bay, Wisconsin, a Rosary Garden was started in 2008 by the members of the parish, led by Marcy Pfeifer. First, Pfeifer designed a Mary Garden. Then she decided to try a Rosary Garden, and everyone in the parish helped plant it. Monsignor Roy Klister, then-rector of the cathedral, was amazed by how quickly the Mary Gardens grew:

> There were 12, 20, or more volunteers, and all of them were bending down, tilling the soil, putting in plants and moving soil. It was a beehive of activity. And all ages. We had people who almost had to have canes to get around, down to those just old enough to barely be able to walk — but carrying a little chunk of dirt from one spot to another, and getting all sorts of praise from mothers and grandmothers. One guy had a tiny little watering pot. His mom showed him where to put the water. He took great pride in pouring that water.

Pfeifer designed a four-level Rosary Garden — one level for each set of the mysteries of the Rosary. The garden is divided into white flowers for the Joyful Mysteries, red for the Sorrowful, gold for the Glorious, and purple for the Luminous.

Pfeifer asked parish members to bring plants from their own homes, such as wood violets (the previously mentioned "Our Lady's modesty") or Lily of the Valley (called "Ladder to Heaven"). While it brought a sense of ownership for people, it also led to some cost savings.

"One older parishioner asked me how we were going to pay for this," Pfeifer recalled. "I said if the good Lord wants a garden for his mother, it will happen."

While flowers and berries hardly seem to have much to do with theology or passing on the Church teachings of the faith, we need to remember that the first place God set human beings on earth was in a garden. The Lord Jesus saved human beings by offering himself for us in another garden. And, finally, he rose from the dead from a tomb in yet one more garden.

Planting a Rosary Garden is not much different from saying a simple repetition of prayers using beads and a piece of string. The garland of prayers that is the Rosary is like a daisy chain sprinkled with roses, sending the scent of devotion up toward heaven, with our prayers rising like incense to the throne.

The poet Elizabeth Barrett Browning could have been speaking of both Mary Gardens and rosaries when she wrote:

Earth is crammed with Heaven, and every common bush afire with God. But only he who sees, takes off his shoes. The rest sit around it and pluck blackberries.[36]

The Rosary, prayed with Mary, reminds us that God in Christ provides all that we need — from fiery glory to wine-filled meals — if we only follow Mary's advice: "Do whatever he tells you" as we reflect on the Gospel message.

And count our beads.

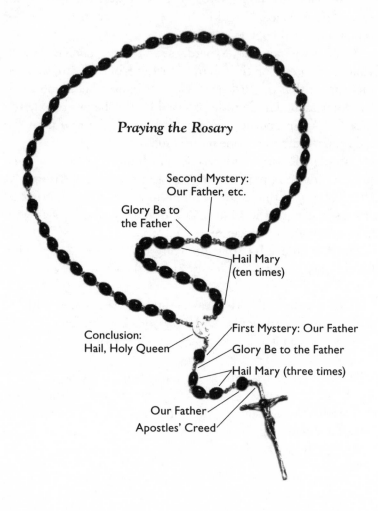

Praying the Rosary

Second Mystery:
Our Father, etc.

Glory Be to
the Father

Hail Mary
(ten times)

Conclusion:
Hail, Holy Queen

First Mystery: Our Father

Glory Be to the Father

Hail Mary (three times)

Our Father

Apostles' Creed

NOTES

1. H. Thurston and A. Shipman. "The Rosary" (1912). In *The Catholic Encyclopedia.* New York: Robert Appleton Company, via New Advent: *http://www.newadvent.org/cathen/13184b.htm.* Accessed July 8. 2009.
2. Ibid.
3. N. 25, *Redemptoris Custos* (*Guardian of the Redeemer*). Pope John Paul II, Aug. 15, 1989. From *www.vatican.va.* Accessed Sept. 14, 2008.
4. Pope John Paul II, Angelus message, Nov. 3, 1996.
5. Rev. Steven Peter Tsichlis, "The Jesus Prayer." From the Greek Orthodox Archdiocese of America, New York, New York: *www.goarch.org.* Accessed July 12, 2009.
6. Rev. M. Basil Pennington, "Prayer," in *The Modern Catholic Encyclopedia.* Michael Glazier and Monica Hellwig, editors (Collegeville, MN: Liturgical Press, 1994).
7. *The Way of a Pilgrim,* translated by R. M. French (New York: Seabury Press, 1965).
8. "Constitution on the Sacred Liturgy" (*Sacrosanctum Concilium*), n. 60. From *http://www.vatican.va/archive/hist_councils/ii_vatican_council/documents/vat-ii_const_19631204_sacrosanctum-concilium_en.html.* Accessed July 12, 2009.
9. C. 1166, *1983 Code of Canon Law.* From *www.vatican.va/archive/ENG1104/_INDEX.HTM.* Accessed July 12, 2009.
10. Ibid.
11. *Baltimore Catechism,* No. 3, Lesson 27, Question 1055.
12. Pope Benedict XVI, Angelus, Sept. 11, 2005. From *http://www.vatican.va/holy_father/benedict_xvi/angelus/2005/documents/hf_ben-xvi_ang_20050911_en.html.* Accessed July 21, 2009.
13. St. Cyril of Jerusalem, *Catecheses,* Lecture 13. From *http://www.newadvent.org/fathers/310113.htm.* Accessed July 21, 2009.
14. Pope Benedict XVI, Homily at Lourdes, France, Sept. 14, 2008. From *http://www.vatican.va/holy_father/benedict_xvi/homilies/2008/documents/hf_ben-xvi_hom_20080914_lourdes-apparizioni_en.html.* Accessed July 21, 2009.
15. *General Instruction of the Roman Missal,* n. 67 (Washington, D.C.: United States Catholic Conference, 2003).
16. Thomas Aquinas, *The Catechetical Instructions.* Rev. Joseph B. Collins, trans. (1939). From *http://www.catholicprimer.org/aquinas/aquinas_catechism.pdf.* Accessed July 21, 2009.
17. "The Martyrdom of Polycarp." Alexander Roberts, and James Donaldson, trans. From *Ante-Nicene Fathers, Vol. 1,* Alexander Roberts, James Donaldson, and A. Cleveland Coxe, eds. (Buffalo, NY: Christian Literature

Publishing Co., 1885). Revised and edited for New Advent by Kevin Knight; *http://www.newadvent.org/fathers/0102.htm*. Accessed Aug. 24, 2009.

18. Pope Paul VI, *Marialis Cultis* (Feb. 2, 1974), n. 45. From *http://www.vatican .va/holy_father/paul_vi/apost_exhortations/documents/hf_p-vi_exh_19740202 _marialis-cultus_en.html*. Accessed Aug. 24, 2009.

19. St. Thérèse of Lisieux, *The Autobiography of St. Thérèse of Lisieux*, Ronald Knox, trans. (New York: P.J. Kennedy and Sons, 1958).

20. *Philippinas Insulas*, p. 419, by Pope Pius XII, *AAS* 38; cited in *Marialis Cultis*. From *www.vatican.va*. Accessed Dec. 28, 2009.

21. *Marialis Cultis*, n. 35. From *www.vatican.va*. Accessed Dec. 28, 2009.

22. Pope John Paul II, *Rosarium Virginis Mariae* (Oct 16, 2002), n. 20. From *www.vatican.va*. Accessed Dec. 28, 2009.

23. Ibid., n. 21.

24. Ibid., n. 19.

25. Ibid., n. 21.

26. *Lumen Gentium*, "Dogmatic Constitution on the Church" (Nov. 21, 1964), n. 31. From *www.vatican.va*. Accessed Dec. 28, 2009.

27. *Sacrosanctum Concilium*, n. 10. From *www.vatican.va*. Accessed Dec. 28, 2009.

28. *Rosarium Virginis Mariae*, n. 40. From *www.vatican.va*. Accessed Dec. 28, 2009.

29. Bishop Frederick Colli, Easter message in *Northwestern Ontario Catholic*, March 2008. From Diocese of Thunder Bay at *www.dotb.ca*. Used with permission. Accessed July 22, 2009.

30. Pope Paul VI, *Marialis Cultis* (Feb. 2, 1974), n. 45. From *www.vatican.va*. Accessed Dec. 28, 2009.

31. Romano Guardini, *The Rosary of Our Lady* (Manchester, NH: Sophia Institute Press, 1999).

32. Father Bernhard Blankenhorn, O.P., Easter Homily, March 23, 2008. From *www.blessed-sacrament.org*. Used with permission. Accessed Dec. 28, 2009.

33. Question 57, Article 6, *Summa Theologica* of St. Thomas Aquinas. From New Advent at *www.newadvent.org*. Accessed Dec. 28, 2009.

34. Nos. 79, 115, "Behold Your Mother: Woman of Faith." Nov. 21, 1973, U.S. Catholic Conference of Bishops. Washington, D.C.

35. Thurston and Shipman, "The Feast of the Assumption." In *The Catholic Encyclopedia* (New York: Robert Appleton Company, 1912). From New Advent: *http://www.newadvent.org/cathen/13184b.htm*. Accessed Sept. 5, 2009.

36. "Aurora Leigh, A Poem," Elizabeth Barrett Browning (London: J. Miller, 1864). Reprinted by Chicago: Academy Chicago Printers (Cassandra Editions), 1979. *http://digital.library.upenn.edu/women/barrett/aurora/aurora.html*. Accessed Dec. 28, 2009.

Index